Pictorial Encyclopedia of Modern JAPAN

Gakken

Pictorial Encyclopedia of Modern JAPAN

Published by GAKKEN CO., LTD.
4-40-5, Kami-ikedai, Ohta-ku, Tokyo 145, Japan

Overseas Distributor : Japan Publications Trading Co., Ltd.
P.O.Box 5030 Tokyo International, Tokyo, Japan.

Distributors :
United States : Kodansha International/USA, Ltd., through Harper & Row, Publishers, Inc., 10 East 53rd Street, New York, N.Y.10022
South America : Harper & Row, Publishers, Inc., International Department
Canada : Fitzhenry & Whiteside Ltd., 195 Allstate Parkway, Markham, Ontario L3R 4T8
British Isles : International Book Distributors Ltd., 66 Wood Lane End, Hemel Hempstead, Herts HP2 4RG
Australia and New Zealand : Bookwise International, 1 Jeanes Street, Beverley, South Australia 5007
The Far East and Japan : Japan Publications Trading Co., Ltd., 1-2-1, Sarugaku-cho, Chiyoda-ku, Tokyo 101

First edition 1986

ISBN : 0-87040-712-0
ISBN : 4-05-150800-5 (in Japan)
Printed in Japan

PREFACE

Japan's technology, industry, business practices, traditional culture—indeed, its very way of life—have become the subjects of intense curiosity as the nation's impact on economic and international affairs makes itself increasingly felt.

As a step toward satisfying that curiosity we have presented here in broad perspective a book that we confidently hope will furnish the general reader with a good close look at those and other aspects of modern Japan. Facts and figures are on every page, and graphs, charts and tables fill a long section at the back of the book. However, it is chiefly through the medium of pictures that we have tried to present the people and industries of Japan, for in keeping with our original intention we wish to show what we are like and to show how our industries reflect and influence our everyday life.

Like ancient Rome, Japan's industry was not built in a day but is, rather, the product of management efforts and hard work spanning an extended period. The industrial structure was formerly one based on heavy chemicals, with huge complexes for steel, petro-chemicals and other industries located around the nation. Subsequent to the two oil crises, however, there has been a shift, so that the processing and assembling industries, by incorporating innovative techniques brought about by the introduction of high technology, have become the mainstream.

The transition from industrial midget to economic giant has resulted in both progress and problems, and it is these that the pictures and text are intended to convey, in the hope that the reader will thus have a clearer understanding of how Japan and its people, like the rest of the world, are coping with and contributing to the development of the modern age in which we live.

Akira Kubota
Richard De Lapp

CONTENTS

Preface   Akira Kubota/Richard De Lapp————3

JAPANESE INDUSTRIES————7
Japan's Economic Development————8
Computers: Machines That Transformed Industry————10
Information Network System(INS)————12
Factory Automation————14
Industrial Machinery Industry————16
The Automobile Industry————18
Japan's Passenger Cars————20
Japanese Motorcycles————26
Consumer Electronics————28
The Computer Industry————30
Progress in Micro-Electronics————32
Precision Instruments————34
Japanese Cameras————36
The Chemical Industry————38
The Medical Drug Industry————40
Cement, Glass and Ceramics Industries————42
Fine Ceramics————44
The Food Industry————46
The Textile Industry————48
Paper, Pulp and Lumber————50
The Steel Industry————52
Shipbuilding————54
Construction and Housing Industries————56
Energy————58
Distribution Diversification————60
Supermarkets and Department Stores————62
Specialty Shops————64
The Shinkansen(Bullet Train) and the Transportation Network————66
The Information Industry————68
The Leisure Industry————70
The Restaurant Industry————72
Agriculture————74
The Forestry Industry————76
The Fishing Industry————78
World Trade————80
Japanese-style Management————82

THE EVERYDAY LIFE OF THE JAPANESE ———— 83

Japanese Houses ————84
Families and Homes ————86
Families and Expenses ————88
The Businessman at Work ————90
The Life of the Businessman ————92
Working Women ————94
Children and the War for Education ————96
The Japanese at Leisure ————98
Urban and Rural Areas ————100
The Old and the New ————102
Festivals ————104
Traditional Industries (1) ————106
Traditional Industries (2) ————108
Population and the Aging of Society ————110
A Safe Japan ————112

JAPAN IN CHARTS AND GRAPHS ———— 113

Farming/Forestry/Water ————114
Mining & Energy ————120
Manufacturing and Construction ————122
Business and Service Industries ————126
World Trade ————128
Population ————130
Pollution/Traffic Accidents/Fires ———— 131
Finance ————132
Prices/Household Finance ————133
Social Security ————134
Education ————136

STAFF

Editorial Consultants
Akira Kubota (Professor of SANNO INSTITUTE ON BUSINESS ADMINISTRATION)
Richard De Lapp
Editorial Staff
Yoshihisa Koyama
Yukio Tachibana
Kisu Production
Book Design
Takushi Shimada

CREDITS

We are grateful to the following for cooperation and permission
to reproduce the photographs:

Asahi Chemical Industry Co Ltd; Asahi Shimbun Publishing Co;
Canon Inc; Casio Co Ltd; Daihatsu Motor Co Ltd; Fanuc Ltd;
Fisheries Agency; Fuji Heavy Industries Ltd; Fuji Photo Film Co Ltd;
Fujitsu Ltd; Hino Motors Ltd; Hitachi Ltd; Hitachi Shipbuilding &
Engineering Co Ltd; Honda Motor Co Ltd; Honshu-Shikoku Bridge
Authority; Iseki & Co Ltd; Isuzu Motors Ltd; Japan International
Cooperation Agency; Japan National Railways; Kao Soap Co Ltd;
Kawasaki Heavy Industries Ltd; Kyocera Corporation; Kyodo News
Service; Kyowa Hakko Kogyo Co Ltd; Matsushita Electric Industrial Co Ltd;
Meteorological Agency; Ministry of Foreign Affairs; Minolta Camera Co Ltd;
Mint Bureau; Misawa Homes Co Ltd; Mitsubishi Heavy Industries Ltd;
Mitsubishi Electric Corporation; Mitsui Mining and Smelting Co Ltd;
National Police Agency; National Research Institute of Police Science;
National Space Development Agency of Japan; Nippondenso Co Ltd;
Nippon Electric Co Ltd; Nippon Hoso Kyokai; Nippon Kogaku K.K.;
Nippon Kokan K.K.; Nippon Reizo K.K.; Nippon Steel Corporation;
Nissan Motor Co Ltd; Noritake Co Ltd; Oji Paper Co Ltd; Olympus Optical
Co Ltd; Pioneer Electric Corporation; Sapporo Breweries Ltd; Sogo Stores
Ltd; Sumitomo Chemical Co Ltd; Sumitomo Electric Industries Ltd;
Takeda Chemical Industries Ltd; The Fuji Bank Ltd; The Furukawa Electric
Co Ltd; The Nikko Securities Co Ltd; The Shin-Etsu Chemical Co Ltd;
The Tokyo Electric Power Co Ltd; Tokyo Broadcasting System Inc;
Toshiba Corporation; TOTO Co Ltd; Toyota Motor Corporation; Victor
Company of Japan Ltd; Yamaha Motor Co Ltd; Yamanouchi Pharmaceutical
Co Ltd; Yamazaki Baking Co Ltd; Gakken Co Ltd (Photo Department).

Jacket and cover photos:Manufacture of Laser-vision Disks
Back cover photo:Light-Fiber Cable

JAPANESE INDUSTRIES

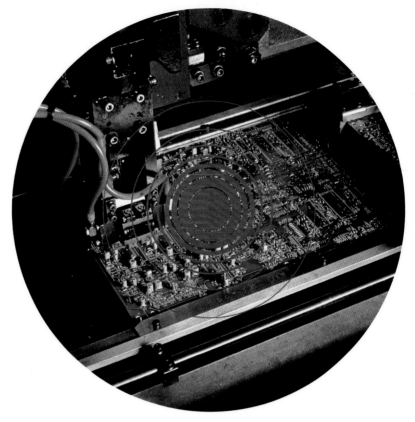

JAPAN'S ECONOMIC DEVELOPMENT

Until around 1965 the label "Made in Japan" carried a connotation of "cheap" or "inferior". Then came the oil shocks of the '70s, bringing major policy changes to Japanese industry, which at that time was 99% dependent on imported oil. The industrial pattern moved from heavy chemicals to industries requiring fewer resources such as the knowledge-intensive industries of electronics, biotechnology, new materials, telecommunications, precision instruments, machine tools, and the trendier ones of apparel and sound equipment.

Japan's industrial products today are totally unlike those of 20 years ago. Areas in which Japan particularly excells are in applications and production, a fact attested to by their internationally competitive edge.

In electronics, biotech and other fields, basic technology is but a step behind America's; yet even here applications and production technology give the nation a worldwide reputation for excellence.

Present problems besetting Japan's economy include competition from developing nations, resource conservation abroad, and trade friction, all of which call for cooperation among the developing and advanced countries of the world.

▲**North Kyushu Industrial Belt** Developed as a heavy chemicals area, with flourishing industries in steel, cement, glass. (Yahata Complex)

Japan's Industrial Belts and Areas

Setouchi Industrial Area

Hokuriku Industrial Area

Chukyo Industrial Belt

Hanshin Industrial Belt

Tokai Industrial Area

Keihin Industrial Belt

North Kyushu Industrial Belt

Keiyo Industrial Area —

▲**Robots at work in a Japanese Factory** NC machines, robots and other industrial machinery are at the basis of Japan's industrial development.

●TECHNOPOLIS

Japan has a number of huge industrial areas (see map), each carrying out important functions. But due to overcrowding, soaring prices for industrial land and other factors, an innovative, intensive pattern of new industrial areas called "Technopolis" is being developed. By attracting non-polluting topline industries, encouraging migration from the cities and promoting regional economic development, the hope is that the Technopolis concept will create a harmonious blend between modern industries and the environment.

▲**Keihin Industrial Belt** In numbers of factories, workers, output, this is Japan's foremost industrial area, producing goods in every field. (Ogishima Complex)

Doo Industrial Area

Kashima Rinkai Industrial Area

▶**Hanshin Industrial Belt** Japan's second leading industrial area. Diverse and export-oriented products include rubber, textiles, matches, bicycles. (Sakai Complex)

▼**Chukyo Industrial Belt** Japan's foremost cloth producer. Cars are also a leading industry. (Nagoya Complex)

COMPUTERS

MACHINES THAT TRANSFORMED INDUSTRY

The computer, developed in America in 1946, has been used for census-taking and missile-tracking, handling huge amounts of data and displaying an awesome ability in complex and enormous calculations.

The development of the IC and the LSI miniaturized computers and improved their capabilities. Used in every field, computers have brought about big changes in society. They are so common in watches, thermometers, TV sets, VCR s, washing machines and cars that new products not using them are increasingly hard to find. Computer banking is now as commonplace as the use of credit cards. In business, they daily collate information from branches to main offices, analyzing and processing it to aid in management and decision-making. Assisted by advances in computergraphics, designers collaborate directly with them, while in factories, robots and NC (Numerically Controlled) machine tool systems engage in various tasks. In medicine, too, equipment such as the CT (Computerized Tomography) scanner has become a necessary tool in the diagnosis of disease. No longer just an indispensable tool, the computer is rapidly finding its way into the educational system to prepare the next generation in its use and operation.

▲ **JNR's Ticketing Service** The Japan National Railway (JNR) has terminals throughout the country to make seat reservations and issue tickets, all controlled by the computer in the head office. The system, initiated in 1960, has grown to handle car rentals, hotel reservations and group tours. Such automated systems are now also spreading among airlines and hotels.

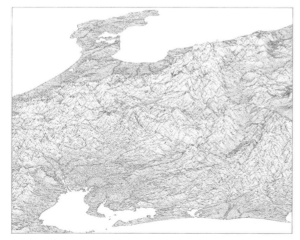

▲ **Map Making** Using data fed into computer, cartographic machine draws map on film or paper.

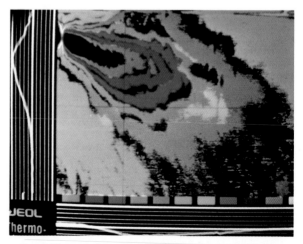

▲ **Room Temperature Distribution** Effectiveness of air-conditioner is checked by computer. Uses are in R&D.

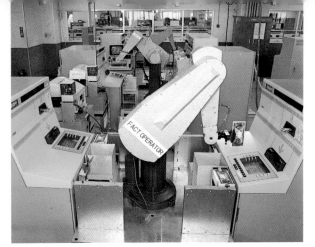

▲**Robot Examiner** Computer-controlled robots test the A.T.M. They work 24 hours a day and perform four times as much work as a man does.

▲**Computer-controlled Car** Pre-programmed with the route, the computer responds to oral commands, shows the way, warns and questions by voice when necessary.

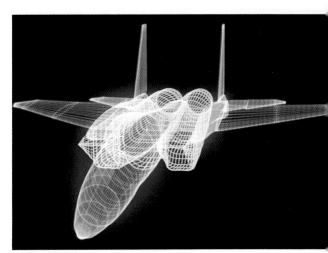

▲**Automatic Weather Station** There are 1,313 of these stations nationwide. Each automatically sends data to the computer in the Meteorological Agency. Collection of data from all stations takes only 10 minutes.

▲**Computer-aided Design of Aircraft** Each part is assembled as a picture on the computer screen. The designer can correct and/or change the data while watching.

●MICROCOMPUTER USES

Without our realizing it, life has become computerized. Items pictured here are but a few of the places where microcomputers are at work.

◀ (left) Microwave oven cooks using data on card
◀ (center) Watch can remember 50 telephone numbers
▼ (below) Keyboard memorizes and plays melodies
▼ (bottom) Thermometer shows temperature in 1 minute

INFORMATION NETWORK SYSTEMS(INS)

Aided by advances in scientific technology, various industries have made rapid gains in products and information exchange so that an advanced information society is now at hand. Playing a major role is the INS, which will gather telephone, digital, facsimile, picture and other transmissions, link home and business to large computers, and utilize satellites to overcome distances, furnishing these services at low cost.

The system will link maker to consumer trends, and efficiently manage shipment, delivery, sales, inventory control, production planning and other operations by computer. Once banking services are added, billing will also be automatic. Called VAN (Value-added Network), the system will operate between business and industry.

Another system, called LAN, will link computers and word processors at workers' desks to a central computer so that data and storage devices can be shared.

When widely in place, such systems will eliminate voluminous paperwork, greatly shorten transaction time between business and industry, and shift pencil-and-paper deskwork to keyboard and display screen, while business meetings via TV and working at home via computer will be common.

▲**Securities Firm Information System** Links center's computer to terminals in subscriber's office or home to furnish up-to-the-minute information.

● INS   First Stage

Sapporo

Kyoto

Fukuoka

Hiroshima

Nagoya

Senda[i]

Tokyo

Osaka

Okinawa

First Stage will link prefectural offices.

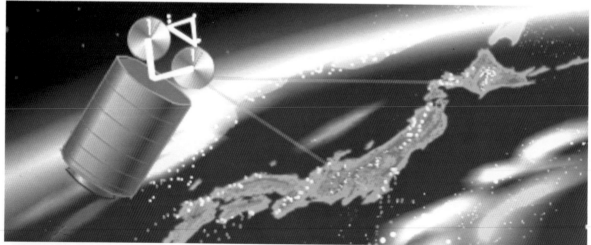

▲**The *YURI* Telecommunications Satellite** Pilot satellite was launched in 1978 but ended in failure. Subsequently re-launched, and is expected to begin operating soon

Photos: Courtesy of Sumitomo Electric Industries Ltd. & Gakken Computer Graphics Center

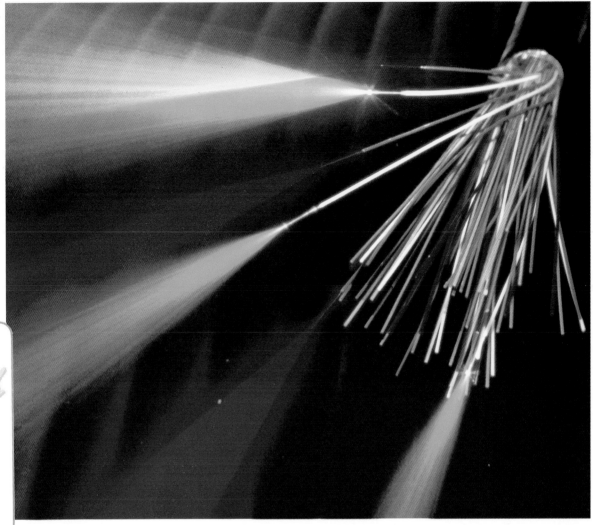

▲**Light Fiber Cable**   A laser beam laden with information passes through a glass fiber only 0.1 mm in diameter. Such cables are widely used in every field.

▼**Office equipped with OA devices**

▼**Televised Conference**   Sound and picture transmissions enable widely separated offices to hold meetings as if in the same room.

FACTORY AUTOMATION

The advent of micro-electronics has enabled man to program industrial robots to perform a wide variety of sophisticated tasks. In turn, this technological advance has intensified the trend toward factories run by computerized robots producing a multitude of high quality goods in mass quantities.

Factory automation is highly advanced in Japan. Reasons include the dearth of a menial labor force due to the homogeneity of the people, and the high wages paid to workers. Toyota, Nissan and other auto makers are good examples, but the prime one is the Fanuc Corporation's factory where materials once delivered to the warehouse are programmed out as needed for manufacturing and assembling into finished products. All deliveries of materials and parts are done by unmanned conveyors, enabling the plant to operate on a 24-hour basis and relieve humans of drudgery and hazardous work.

Even in such an "unmanned" factory, however, man is still there, for it is man who must create and input the programs for the robots. His place has simply shifted from the workfloor to the central control room where he oversees the entire production process.

▲ **Manufacturing Plant**   Robots and NC units all lined up. Unmanned conveyors in central aisle bring materials as needed and take finished items to automated warehouse.

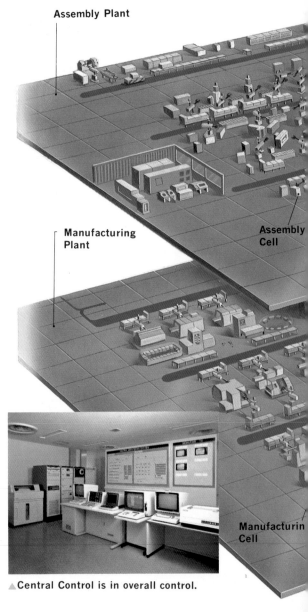

Assembly Plant

Manufacturing Plant

Assembly Cell

Manufacturin Cell

▼ **Assembly Cell**   After one robot takes parts from unmanned conveyor and sets them in designated spots, another robot assembles them.

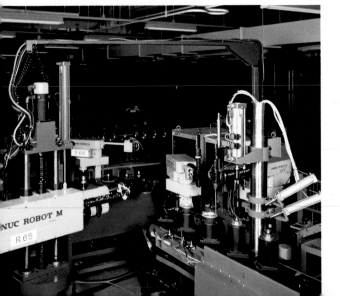

NUC ROBOT M
R 65

▲ **Central Control is in overall control.**

▲ Low need for workers enabled Fanuc to build its plant in a farming community (pop. 6000) near Mt. Fuji.

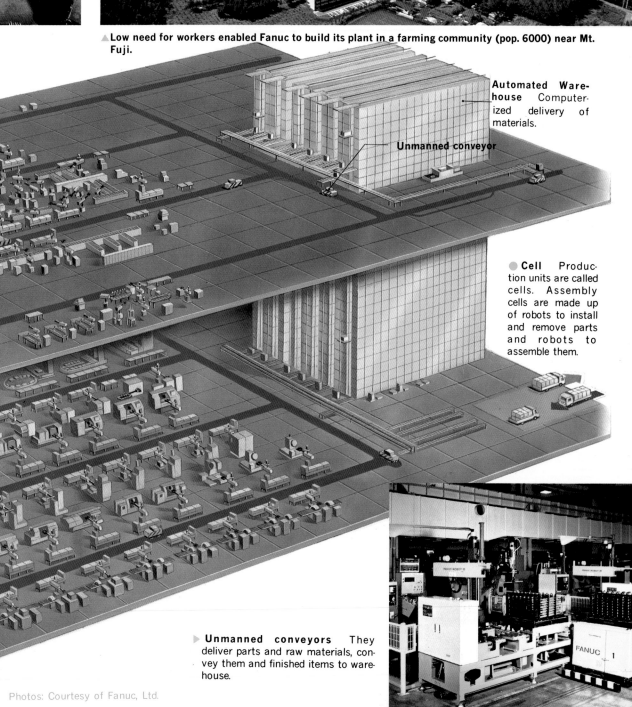

Automated Warehouse Computerized delivery of materials.

Unmanned conveyor

● **Cell** Production units are called cells. Assembly cells are made up of robots to install and remove parts and robots to assemble them.

▶ **Unmanned conveyors** They deliver parts and raw materials, convey them and finished items to warehouse.

INDUSTRIAL MACHINERY INDUSTRY

Japanese industry and industrial machinery more or less developed in tandem. In basic research and technology, Japan is a step behind America and Europe, but in applications and production, especially in mass production techniques, the nation's technology is at the forefront worldwide. Supporting it is industrial machinery.

Reaping the results of rapid advances in electronics technology are a number of devices which, in Japan, are referred to as "mecha-tronics" (*mecha*nism + elec*tronics*). Representative examples are NC machines and industrial robots.

Such devices have had a strong impact, and have widely automated production facilities in Japan. In offices, electronic applications have changed the nature of many office machines, as computers, once used primarily for calculating now handle word and information processing. Factories have their industrial robots, offices their electronics equipment, all helping to automate work and make it more efficient. The same forces are at work in many other industrial sectors.

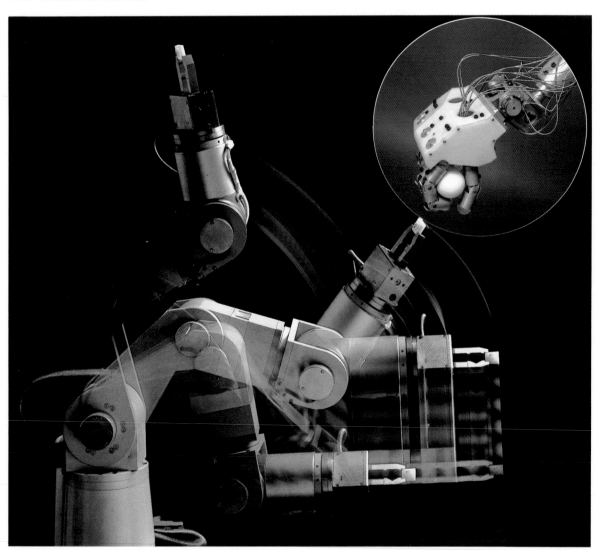

▲**Multi-jointed Robot**   Able to grasp extremely small objects and move them to designated places with precision.

▲**Robot Using Shape-memory Alloy**   Movement is like that of human muscle. (inset)

Photos: Courtesy of FURUKAWA ELECTRIC & FUJITSU Ltd.

■MAIN INDUSTRIAL ROBOTS

▲**Machine Processing Robot**   Robot (front center) affixes item to be made to NC unit (behind), removing it after processing is completed.

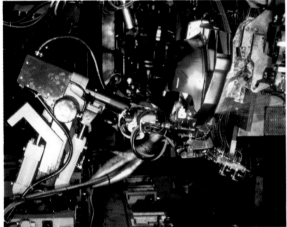

▲**Spot-Welding Robot**   Works mainly with thin sheet-metal. Photo: Welding car body.

▲**Painter Robot**   Once programmed, it executes tasks unfailingly and repeatedly, spray-painting car body.

▼**Assembly Robot**   Equipped with "vision" it distinguishes shapes, checks positions, then assembles.

▼**Injection-molding Robot**   Makes plastic items ranging from daily goods to car parts, all of uniform quality.

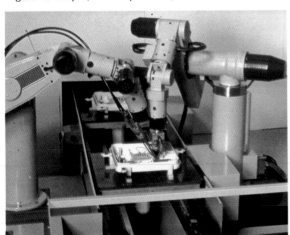

THE AUTOMOBILE INDUSTRY

The Japanese auto industry grew rapidly after 1955 under the combined impetus of domestic demand and expanded exports, by-passing West Germany in 1967 and America in 1980 to find itself in the front rank in production and exports. Car ownership ranks next to America's, and the industry is an important foreign-currency earner.

Factors contributing to the high growth after the oil crisis include : (1) the slowness of American makers in gearing up for compact cars, (2) the reputation earned by Japanese compacts for superior economy, quality and service, and (3) the early investment in automation, robotics, and computer-aided design.

Excessive exports of Japanese cars have led to boycotts in, and economic friction with, many nations. Yet the industry's organization and quality control systems are the focus of worldwide attention, and exports of technology, tie-ups with major foreign makers and production in both America and Europe are under way.

▲ **Forging** Essential engine parts are forged and processed using modern equipment.

▲ **Engine Assembly** Cylinder head, crankshaft and other precision parts are assembled.

▲ **Giant Presses** Stamp out body parts and sections from pre-set lengths of steel.

▲ **Control Room** A computer monitors, checks, adjusts and controls the flow and condition of each step in the manufacturing process.

▲ **Shower Test** With the final test completed, cars are given a high-pressure shower to check for leakage, then shipped to dealers.

Photos: Courtesy of Toyota Motor Corporation.

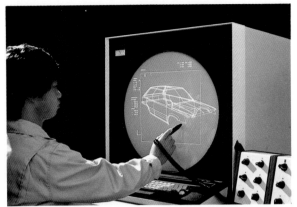

▲**Car Design**   Computer-assisted design (CAD), numerous idea sketches and clay models are some of the many processes involved in the search for the ideal car.

▲**Wind Tunnel Test**   Repeatedly carrying out tests under various conditions yields data from which better cars are produced.

▲**Body Assembly**   Body parts move down assembly line to be spot-welded by robots.

▲**Painting**   Done by robots at the painting plant. Painting is for appearance as well as for rust prevention.

▲**Final Test**   Assembled car undergoes final testing and adjustments of brakes, axle, instrument panel and exhaust gas.

▲**Body Mount**   Accelerator and engine are attached to the finished body, completing the car assembly.

JAPAN'S PASSENGER CARS

● Not all cars are exported.
● Some cars retain the Japanese name

Guide ①Length ②Width ③Weight
④Passenger Capacity ⑤Engine ⑥Drive

■ Standard Cars(2000C C+)

NISSAN PRESIDENT

①5.280m ②1.830m ③1980kg
④5 ⑤4414cc, 200hp ⑥FR

NISSAN CEDRIC

①4.860m ②1.720m ③1475kg
④5 ⑤2960cc, 180hp ⑥FR

TOYOTA SOARER

①4.675m ②1.695m ③1305kg
④5 ⑤2759cc, 175hp ⑥FR

TOYOTA CROWN

①4.860m ②1.720m ③1500kg
④5 ⑤2759cc, 175hp ⑥FR

MITSUBISHI DEBONAIR EXECUTIVE

①4.670m ②1.690m ③1385kg
④5 ⑤2555cc, 220hp ⑥FR

Photos: Courtesy of Nissan Motor Co., Ltd., Toyota Motor Corporation, Mitsubishi Motor Co., Ltd. & Mazda K.K.

■Compacts(2000C C & under)

MAZDA 626

①4.515m ②1.690m ③1040kg
④5 ⑤1998cc, 120hp ⑥FF

TOYOTA CRESSIDA (MARK II)

①4.670m ②1.690m ③1245kg
④5 ⑤1988cc, 160hp ⑥FR

MITSUBISHI ETERNA Λ

①4.570m ②1.675m ③1250kg
④5 ⑤1997cc, 145hp ⑥FR

NISSAN LAUREL

①4.675m ②1.690m ③1195kg
④5 ⑤1998cc, 125hp ⑥FR

NISSAN SKYLINE

①4.620m ②1.675m ③1245kg
④5 ⑤1990cc, 205hp ⑥FR

MAZDA 929

①4.665m ②1.690m ③1135kg
④5 ⑤1998cc, 120hp ⑥FR

MITSUBISHI GALANT

①4.660m ②1.695m ③1180kg
④5 ⑤1997cc, 200hp ⑥FF

MAZDA LUCE

①4.690m ②1.690m ③1125kg
④5 ⑤573cc×2, 130hp ⑥FR

TOYOTA CHASER

①4.670m ②1.690m ③1245kg
④5 ⑤1988cc, 125hp ⑥FR

ISUZU IMPULSE (PIAZZA)

①4.310m ②1.655m ③1155kg
④5 ⑤1949cc, 135hp ⑥FR

NISSAN SANTANA

①4.545m ②1.690m ③1150kg
④5 ⑤1994cc, 110hp ⑥FF

NISSAN LEOPARD TR·X

①4.630m ②1.690m ③1255kg
④5 ⑤1998cc, 125hp ⑥FR

NISSAN 200SX (SILVIA)

①4.430m ②1.660m ③1170kg
④5 ⑤1990cc, 150hp ⑥FR

ISUZU ASKA

①4.440m ②1.670m ③1085kg
④5 ⑤1995cc, 89hp ⑥FF

MAZDA RX·7

①4.320m ②1.670m ③1000kg
④4 ⑤573cc×2, 130hp ⑥FR

TOYOTA SUPRA (CELICA)

①4.660m ②1.685m ③1255kg
④5 ⑤2759cc, 175hp ⑥FR

HONDA CIVIC COUPE CR·X

①3.675m ②1.625m ③800kg
④4 ⑤1488cc, 110hp ⑥FF

NISSAN 300ZX   (FAIRLADY Z)

①4.335m ②1.725m ③1325kg
④2 ⑤2960cc, 230hp ⑥FR

HONDA PRELUDE

①4.295m　②1.690m　③980kg
④4　⑤1829cc, 125hp　⑥FF

TOYOTA CORONA

①4.505m　②1.665m　③1175kg
④5　⑤1770cc, 160hp　⑥FR

ISUZU I-MARK (GEMNI)

①4.245m　②1.570m　③1015kg
④5　⑤1817cc, 73hp　⑥FR

HONDA VIGOR

①4.255m　②1.665m　③980kg
④5　⑤1829cc, 110hp　⑥FF

SUBARU LEONE

①4.370m　②1.660m　③1395kg
④5　⑤1781cc, 135hp　⑥FF+4WD

HONDA ACCORD

①4.255m　②1.665m　③960kg
④5　⑤1829cc, 110hp　⑥FF

MITSUBISHI LANCER EX

①4.225m　②1.620m　③1085kg
④5　⑤1795cc, 160hp　⑥FR

NISSAN MAXIMA

①4.500m　②1.690m　③1090kg
④5　⑤1809cc, 135hp　⑥FF

MITSUBISHI CORDIA

①4.395m　②1.665m　③1030kg
④5　⑤1795cc, 135hp　⑥FF

TOYOTA CELICA

①4.435m　②1.665m　③1155kg
④5　⑤1770cc, 160hp　⑥FR

TOYOTA COUPE GTS

①4.135m　②1.635m　③870kg
④5　⑤1587cc, 100hp　⑥FR

TOYOTA CAROLLA Sport

①4.205m　②1.625m　③940kg
④5　⑤1587cc, 130hp　⑥FR

TOYOTA CARINA

①4.390m　②1.665m　③1110kg
④5　⑤1587cc, 130hp　⑥FR

NISSAN PULSAR

①4.095m　②1.620m　③910kg
④5　⑤1487cc, 115hp　⑥FF

MITSUBISHI MIRAGE

①4.005m　②1.635m　③835kg
④5　⑤1468cc, 87hp　⑥FF

HONDA CIVIC

①3.810m　②1.630m　③815kg
④5　⑤1488cc, 100hp　⑥FF

MAZDA 323

①3.955m　②1.630m　③825kg
④5　⑤1490cc, 85hp　⑥FF

NISSAN SENTRA

①4.135m　②1.640m　③800kg
④5　⑤1487cc, 85hp　⑥FF

HONDA CITY

①3.380m　②1.570m　③670kg
④5　⑤1231cc, 67hp　⑥FF

TOYOTA STARLET

①3.760m　②1.530m　③740kg
④5　⑤1290cc, 74hp　⑥FR

　Photos: Courtesy of Toyota Motor Corporation, Nissan Motor Co., Ltd., Mitsubishi Motor Co., Honda Motor Co., Ltd.,

NISSAN MICRA

①3.785m ②1.560m ③635kg
④5 ⑤987cc, 57hp ⑥FF

SUBARU JUSTY

①3.535m ②1.535m ③700kg
④5 ⑤997cc, 63hp ⑥4WD

DAIHATSU CHARADE

①3.550m ②1.550m ③685kg
④5 ⑤993cc, 80hp ⑥FF

■ Subcompacts (550cc & under)

DAIHATSU CUORE

①3.195m ②1.395m ③580kg
④4 ⑤547cc, 31hp ⑥FF

MITSUBISHI MINICA

①3.195m ②1.395m ③580kg
④4 ⑤546cc, 42hp ⑥FF

SUZUKI CERVO

①3.195m ②1.395m ③550kg
④4 ⑤543cc, 29hp ⑥FF

SUBARU REX

①3.195m ②1.395m ③570kg
④4 ⑤544cc, 31hp ⑥FF

▽ **Twin Cam 24-Valve Engine**
(Based on the prize-winning 1G-GEU)
Attains high-level output while retaining the smoothness and quietness inherent in the in-line 6-cylinder engine design.

▲**Dashboard (Toyota Soarer)**   Graphs and digital indicators
illuminate the instrument panel.

JAPANESE MOTORCYCLES

Japan's producers of two-wheeled vehicles take pride in their worldwide-high production, exports and domestic owner-ship, which make them the world leader.

By origin and tradition a product of Europe, the motorcycle led Japan's motorization after World War II and attained a rapid growth.

That period was also the time that saw many makers, both foreign and domestic, vanish from the scene as a result of technological competition. There are at present in Japan four makers (Honda, Yamaha, Suzuki, Kawasaki), who control the world market in motorcycles.

▲ **Motorcycle Shipment** Vying with Harley-Davidson and BMW, Japan's motorcycles are enjoying worldwide attention.

Data

①Length ②Weight ③Engine

▶HONDA CBX750F
①2.145m
②217kg
③4cycle, 4stroke
   747cc, 77hp

▶HONDA CBX650
①2.160m
②197kg
③4cycle, 4stroke
   655cc, 45hp

◀YAMAHA XZ400D
①2.135m
②200kg
③4cycle, 2stroke
   398cc, 45hp

▶SUZUKI RG250γ HB
①2.050m
②128kg
③2cycle, 2stroke
   247cc, 45hp

◀KAWASAKI AR125
①2.015m
②98kg
③2cycle, 1stroke
   123cc, 22hp

▶YAMAHA TOWN MATE 50
①1.850m
②75kg
③4cycle, 1stroke
   49cc, 5hp

YAMAHA TZR250
① 2.095
② 165kg
③ 2cycle, 2stroke
　 247cc 45hp

HONDA TLM200R
① 2.010
② 92kg
③ 2cycle, 1stroke
　 193cc, 13hp

YAMAHA YZR500
① 2.085
② 194kg
③ 2cycle
　 499cc, 64hp

HONDA ATC250R
① 1.905m
② 131kg
③ 2cycle, 1stroke
　 346cc, 39hp

SUZUKI   RAN
① 1.505m
② 44kg
③ 2cycle, 1stroke
　 49cc, 4.0hp

HONDA   GYRO-X
① 1.635m
② 81kg
③ 2cycle, 1stroke
　 49cc, 5.0hp

HONDA   GORILLA
① 1.365m
② 59kg
③ 4cycle, 1stroke
　 49cc, 2.6hp

YAMAHA   PASSOL
① 1.515m
② 42kg
③ 2cycle, 1stroke
　 49cc, 2.3hp

CONSUMER ELECTRONICS

Japanese makers of electronic and electric products enjoy a practically overwhelming position in the world today. In attaining it, an important milestone was the first telecast in 1953. By 1957, the industry was set up for production, output doubled in each succeeding year, and by year-end in 1961, 80% of homes in Japan had a TV. Color was first telecast in 1960. By 1968, unit production replaced black-and-white. With diffusion at the saturation point, second or third sets are now in the home. Choices range from large-screen to pocket TVs with high-definition TV ready and waiting for the first telecast.

VCRs first appeared around 1975. The '80s are seeing advances in video disks and the digital audio compact disk, the so-called forerunner of the audio revolution. Diffusion for video disks stood at 3% in 1985. Improvements in video cameras are also coming fast: auto-focus, more compact and lighter. An 8mm video camera developed in 1985 weighs less than 1 kilogram.

▲**From Tapes to Disks** In the unceasing search for improvements in sound, picture and convenience, the Japanese market is changing from audio tape to compact disk. from VCR to video disk. (Photo: aluminum coating being applied to laser-vision disks.)

▲**Computer-aided Design** At the planning stage the computer is fed data on design, function and assembly, to aid in the design of a device or system.

▲**Video Insert Machine** Assembly work, right down to fine details, is done by robot, which performs even complex work with both speed and accuracy.

▲**VCR Automatic Deck-Assembly** Computer-controlled machine attaches motor head, parts, and assembles deck.

●VCR PRODUCTION

Video Cassette Recorder (VCR) production requires advanced electronics, precision work and assembly know-how. A representative Japanese export, VCRs are mainly exported to America and the EC nations.

▶**Chassis Assembly** The VCR microprocessor, terminal and various other parts are attached and connected.
▼**Final Inspection** Checks and adjustments are made to screen, color, sound, record and play functions, and close scrutiny given to appearance and safety features.

THE COMPUTER INDUSTRY

The computer only goes back to 1946, when the first one was completed in America. Japan built a test model in 1957, and within a short span became a leading producer, with products from the industry currently being used in offices, factories, the home and elsewhere.

Although IBM holds some 60% of the computer market worldwide, the high-tech level of Japanese makers is rapidly improving, the gap with IBM is closing, the Japanese share of the domestic market continues to rise, and exports are on a sharp increase.

Keeping pace with computer advances are such peripherals for home electronics as floppy disks, compact disks, and display equipment, while in industry and business there have been such dazzling developments in telecommunication systems and OA technology that telephone equipment, facsimile machines, personal computers, word processors and copiers are bringing about near-revolutionary changes in each and every field. Also underway since 1982 with government cooperation is R&D of next-generation (Artificial Intelligence) computers with perception, reasoning and judging abilities.

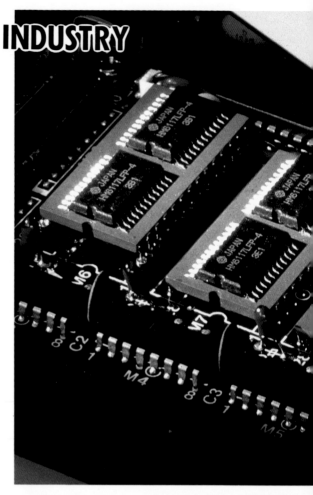

▲**HEMT (High Electron Mobility Transistor)** Development in Japan of the HEMT has excited interest in it as a device for future high-speed computers.

▲**Computer Test-line** Assembled computers are subjected to a variety of robot-administered checks as they near completion.

 Photos: Courtesy of Kyocera Corporation & Fujitsu, Ltd.

▲ Software Development An automatic translation sys -
tem for Japanese to English and vice versa was an-
nounced in 1984. The spread of hardware underscores
the need for a speed-up in software development.

▲ Super Computer Makers of computers capable of high-
speed calculations number only seven worldwide, including
three Japanese firms.

**▲ Multi-layer Type Ceramic Packages Used in the Heart of
the Portable Computer** IC development as well as input
and output equipment in Japan is on a par with America's
and accounts for a large share of the world market. Work
is presently underway in Japan on Fifth Generation computers capable of reasoning and understanding natural
speech.

●TYPES OF COMPUTERS

▼ Large-scale Computers Used for
train reservations, weather foreca-
sting and banking services.

▼ Medium-scale Computers Used
in laboratories and firms.

▼ Small-scale Computers
Mostly for personal use.

PROGRESS IN MICRO-ELECTRONICS

The history of the computer can also be called the history of the semi-conductor. The first computer built was in America in 1946, used 18,000 vacuum tubes and occupied an entire floor. In 1948, a transistor to replace the vacuum tube was invented at Bell Telephone Laboratories. It was a device that used two wires in contact with a germanium slab. After development, progress came rapidly, and in 1954 germanium was replaced by silicon, bringing us to the IC (integrated circuit) stage of today. The IC, an electronic circuit built on a small silicon chip about 5mm × 5mm, consists of many transistors, diodes and other electronic parts.

The first IC in Japan was made in 1961, and consisted of less than 10 parts. Today, ICs of 100,000 to 1,000,000 parts, called LSI (large scale IC)are being developed. Once put into practical use, the LSI will reduce the large-scale computers of today into suitcase size and take the use of the computer into every field, including the home, as part of the computer revolution, in which the Japanese industry intends to take a major role.

▼**Micro-computer Wafer**　Areas using wafers are swiftly expanding due to progress in IC and LSI developmental technology stemming from advanced processing techniques and applications.

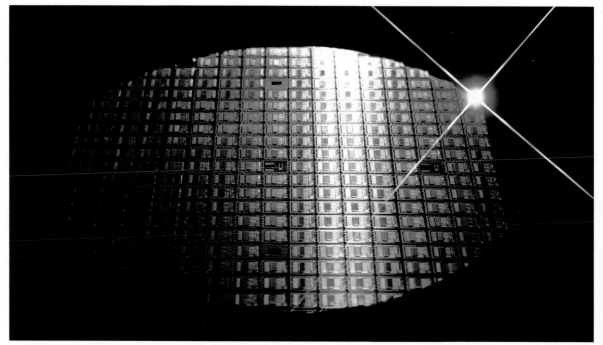

　Photos: Courtesy of Olympus Optical Co., Ltd., Kyocera Corporation, Fujitsu, Ltd. & Mitsubishi Electric Corporation.

▲**Metallic Coating Test by Stepper**   Japan is slightly behind America in basic R&D but on a par in production techniques. Tests and research on the development of LSI and even larger LSI are repeatedly being carried out.

▲**LSI Design**   Some 2.5 million elements are put onto the surface of a silicon chip no larger than 5mm^2. Such advances in machines that produce these semiconductors have been a major factor in the development of Japan's semiconductor industry.

▼**Multi-layer Type IC Packages**   Large-scale production of these inexpensive, high-reliability devices has been made possible by advances in production techniques. Japanese makers of this type of ceramic package will dominate the world market.

▲**Exposing of Super LSI**   Circuit patterns of over I million elements are exposed on a minute silicon wafer. The process is so ultra-precise that a dust particle of even less than 0.1 micron must be guarded against.

▲**Three-Dimensional Integrated Circuit**   ICs now come in layers. With Japan the only nation taking them up in earnest, there are high hopes for practical applications.

PRECISION INSTRUMENTS

In pre-war Japan this industry attained a high level due to military necessity, especially in the watch and camera fields. After the war, these technologies were applied to peacetime industries and advanced rapidly in the '50s and '60s, catching up with, then passing, the Swiss in watchmaking and the West Germans in cameras.

With the advent of electronics, a major change occurred in these industries. Overnight, digital watches gave a new image to the wristwatch. In 1973, Seiko came out with its digital quartz watch and was followed almost immediately by other established firms plus newcomers to the field.

Konica, in 1977, put its automatic focus camera on the market. Other makers soon followed suit, to the extent that these cameras have become the industry's mainstay, a position previously held by the reflex camera.

Both the watchmaking and camera industries have diversified, producing various machines for the medical and business fields. Canon, the maker in Japan with the highest sales, has had more growth in its copiers and desk calculators than in its camera division.

Through the application of electronics, other fields in the industry (water and gas meters, precision scales, etc.) are also making solid progress.

●PROCESS OF MAKING CAMERAS

①Production of optical glass ②Grinding and polishing of lens ③Automatic centering of lens

⑦Finished lens machine-check ⑧Production of camera body ⑨Attaching parts to the body

①Shutter Button
②Film Wind Lever
③Shutter Speed Dial
④Finder
⑤Rewind Knob
⑥Lens Mount
⑦Positioning Hole
⑧PC Socket
⑨Lens Interchange
⑩Light Sensor
⑪Integrated Circuit
⑫Film Rewind Button
⑬Battery Room
⑭Tripod Socket
⑮Flexible Print Board

④Individual inspection of lens ⑤Coating to reduce reflection ⑥Lens assembly and adjustment

⑩Soldering of precision parts ⑪Adjustment of shutter speed ⑫Final camera-check

JAPANESE CAMERAS

● 35mm SLRs

● Not all cameras are exported.
● Some cameras retain the Japanese name.

Olympus OM-4
35mm SLR incorporating a spot meter

Nikon FA
More accuracy through automatic exposure multi-pattern metering

Canon F-1
35mm SLR for professional photographers

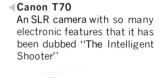

Nikon F3
35mm SLR heavy duty camera for professional use

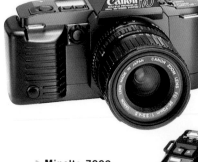

Canon T70
An SLR camera with so many electronic features that it has been dubbed "The Intelligent Shooter"

Contax 159MM
35mm SLR with shutter speed 1/4000 sec and X(1/250 sec) flash synchro.

Minolta 7000
Auto SLR adopting a full-fledged auto focus mechanism

Contax RTS II Quartz
SLR developed jointly by Carl Zeiss and Yashika

Minolta 9000
Model 7000 camera upgraded to professional specifications

●Compact Cameras

◀Canon Auto Boy2
The most popular of the compacts

▲Olympus XA3
Ultra-small 35mm compact camera

◀Fuji HD-M
All-weather camera useable in water up to 2m deep

▶Fuji TW300
Compact camera capable of zoom and wide-angle

Nikon L35AD2 (One · Touch)
Nikon 35mm compact camera

●Underwater Camera

◀Nikonos-V
Full-fledged underwater camera utilizing TTL metering

●Instant Camera

◀Fuji Instant Camera 800AF
Auto focus camera that uses ISO800 instant film

●6×7 SLRs

◀Zenza Bronica GS-1
Advanced electronic 6X7 format lens shutter SLR camera

▼Mamiya RZ67
6X7 format SLR with various interchangeable lenses and accessories

Kyocera Corporation, Bronica Co., Ltd., Mamiya Camera Co., Ltd. & Minolta Camera Co., Ltd.

37

THE CHEMICAL INDUSTRY

The chemical industry makes many of the basic raw materials for other industries as well as consumer end-products. It thus has a direct bearing on the basics of food, clothing and shelter.

Raw materials for the industry include salt, carbide, coal, petroleum, natural gas and fats and oils. After the war, petroleum superceded coal as the most important item and grew rapidly after 1960. A positive application of foreign technology brought the industry remarkable advances and established it as the foremost materials-industry second only to steel. Simultaneously, it overtook W. Germany and is next to America in the production of key products.

In the '70s, however, the role of the industry in environmental pollution became a problem of social concern. Also, soaring oil costs, widening price margins with foreign firms and expanded facilities abroad have meant export cutbacks and import increases. Since the products division, with its engineering plastics and fine chemicals, is more lucrative than the materials division, more and more companies are coming to weigh the possibilities of shifting over to manufacturing.

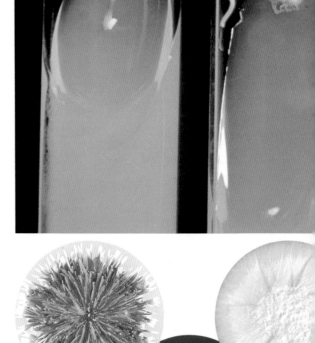

▼The Kashima petrochemical complex

Engineering Plastics These materials are so superior in heat and water resistance and dimensional stability that they are ideal for use in electronics, cars and medical equipment.

Germination From a Callus Plants can be reproduced by tissue-culturing a single cell. Great stress is currently being placed on biotechnological R&D of cell cultivation, gene splicing and cell fusion. Developments in new drugs, plant breeding and the biological computer are also helping to make the field flower as a bio-industry.

Cultivation of Microorganisms Biotechnology is changing these organisms into useful ones. The microbe used in fermentation will be used in antibiotics, food and pesticides.

Epoxy Resins Uses are wide, as in paints and adhesives. New usages will be in sealing ICs.

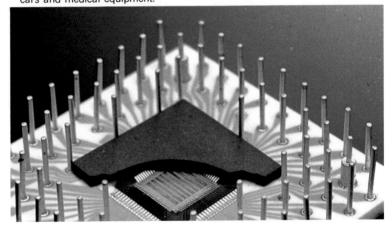

Paint Factory Oil-based paints are gradually being superceded by those made from synthetic materials.

Magnetic Tape Cutter Polyester film is given a magnetic coating and then cut.

Photos: Courtesy of Kyowa Hakko Kogyo Co., Ltd & Sumitomo Chemical Co., Ltd.

THE MEDICAL DRUG INDUSTRY

The drug industry is classified as belonging to the chemical industry, as the manufacturing process is similar. Governmental control, however, is extremely strict, since the industry's products are used in the diagnosis, treatment and prevention of human and animal illnesses.

Drugs can only be made with the permission of the Ministry of Health and Welfare. Also, each step in the manufacturing process must have the Ministry's approval. Additionally, drugs already on the market are subject to reevaluation at the discretion of the Ministry.

The growth of the industry has been stupendous since 1961 when national health insurance coverage took effect. Of the three categories of drugs (for doctors to administer, for drugstores to dispense, and those for home consumption), drugs to be administered by doctors have shown the most growth, mainly due to the insurance system with its universal coverage which allows anyone to consult a doctor and insures that the doctor will be paid.

The progress made in pharmacology and medicine during the same 20 years is reflected in the drug industry, which has produced a succession of new drugs and risen to a top position worldwide in terms of new-drug development. The task for the industry today is to bring its power to bear on cancer and other diseases that afflict mankind.

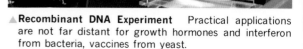

▲**Recombinant DNA Experiment**   Practical applications are not far distant for growth hormones and interferon from bacteria, vaccines from yeast.

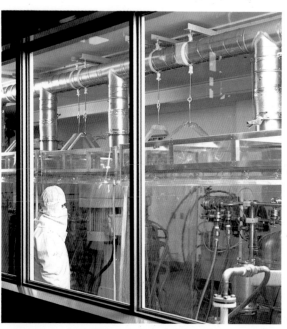

▲**Interferon Experiment**   Experiments aided by genetic engineering to mass-produce interferon as a weapon against cancer are drawing worldwide attention.

●MEDICAL ENGINEERING

Ultrasonic Diagnosis and the CT Scanner (Computerized Tomography) are two important examples of modern diagnostic equipment. Also of increasing value in both diagnosis and treatment are radiation and laser rays. Artificial organs too are being steadily developed and improved, while other marvels of medical engineering that are helping to computerize the entire field of medical care are computer-aided diagnosis and practical applications of IC cards.

▼Artificial bones and joints made of fine ceramics.

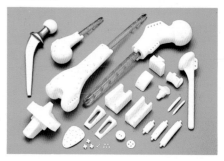

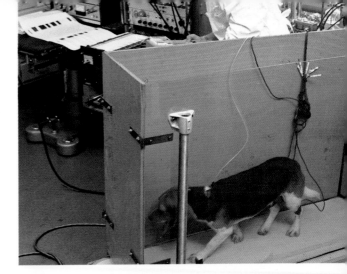

▲ Injections are prepared in a sterile room where super-clean air keeps them free from foreign matter and germs. Workers are dressed from head to toe in sterile suits.

▶ Experiments for R&D of new drugs require at least two different kinds of animals for exacting tests to determine effectiveness and safety.

▶ Visual examination eliminates broken and irregular tablets.

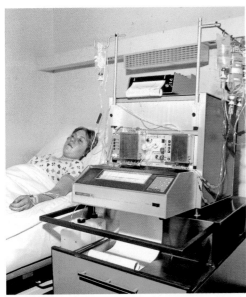

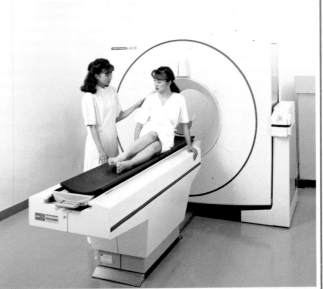

▲ Artificial pancreas automatically measures blood-sugar levels and supplies insulin accordingly.

▲ The CT Scanner makes cross-section X-rays of an affected area and is a powerful aid in the diagnosis of brain tumors, cerebral hemorrhage, heart disease and other disorders.

CEMENT, GLASS AND CERAMICS INDUSTRIES

These industries use raw materials from the ground (clay, rock, limestone, etc.), processing them in high-temperature kilns. Cement, glass and ceramics are the main products. Others include plugs, insulators and enamelware.

Cement is widely used in construction, and with Japan's abundance of limestone, plus the demands of public works, cement output ranks only behind the USSR.

The glass industry is roughly separated into plate glass and glassware. The former needs a high technology that has put Japan next to America in terms of output.

The ceramics industry developed through exports and is tied to the localities that produce its raw materials. Its R&D of fine ceramics holds out a bright future.

▲**Cement Plant**　Large cylinders are rotary kilns.

▲**Potter's Wheel**　Once the clay has been thoroughly kneaded it is put on the wall and spun to form a shape. Baking follows. (Hagi-ware)

▲**Painting**　Painting is done after the initial baking. Colors and designs are unique to the type of pottery. (Arita-ware)

● **Glass and Pottery Products**

▲**District in Shinjuku** Vast amounts of plate glass are used to obtain the desired lightness and sharpness in design.

▼**Figured Plateglass Production** A glass ribbon passes between rollers to receive pattern imprints.

▲**Tile Factory**

▼**Manufacture of porcelain bathroom fixtures**

FINE CERAMICS

Fine ceramics are new materials bringing big changes to our lives. Able to withstand 1800°C and able to be finely processed, fine ceramics in the form of tile covered the outer surface of the Space Shuttle. More heat-resistant than metals or plastic, they also stand up better to acid or alkali, are extremely hard and will not wear.

With such properties, fine ceramics are generating unprecedented new products. Knives, scissors and other cutting tools made of them are nearly as hard as diamonds, do not wear, rust or lose their sharpness.

Due to the heat resistance of fine ceramics, engine applications will mean doing away with coolers and using the heat to advantage elsewhere.

Fine ceramics are also at the core of a great number of electrical products and are used as the base for ICs and LSIs. It was fine ceramics that enabled calculators to become small and more efficient.

Medical science is also benefiting from fine ceramics. Artificial bones and teeth are made from them, with the latter able to withstand tremendous pressure and having no ill effects on the body.

For Japan, a country rich in ceramics, this new type holds great prospects.

▲**Calcinatory**   Materials highly refined for the desired degree of purity are given shape by pressing or other means and then calcined to produce a finished product.

▲**Car Engine**   The heat-resistance of fine ceramics makes them ideal for use in engines.

▲**Cutting Tool**   Fine ceramics materials are so hard and heat-resistant that they can be used for the cutting work done on a lathe.

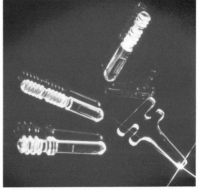

▲**Artificial Tooth Root**   R&D of fine ceramics includes uses as teeth, bones and other medical applications.

▼**Jewelry**   Another of the many applications of fine ceramics is that for jewelry. (Photo: black opal)

▲**Surface Acoustic Wave (SAW) Filters** used in the most sophisticated of TV sets.

THE FOOD INDUSTRY

The changing dietary habits of the Japanese in recent years have seen a corresponding growth in industries for Chinese, Japanese and western-style food products.

Whereas the Japanese products are mainly produced by small and medium-size companies around the nation, non-Japanese foods are more apt to be mass-produced by large firms. Their growth rate is also faster.

With agriculture and livestock at the basis of the food industry, Japan cannot compete internationally. Thus, trade liberalization since the 1960s has meant increased imports of raw materials and dependence on market movements abroad, much to the detriment of some firms, although others have begun to go abroad in search of cheaper raw materials.

▲**Soy Sauce** This peculiarly Japanese flavoring is made from soybeans, wheat, salt and other ingredients which are fermented and allowed to age 1-2 years. Photo shows a traditional way to make soy sauce.

●MAKING BREAD

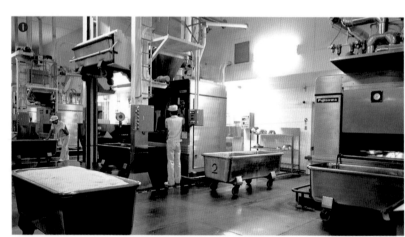

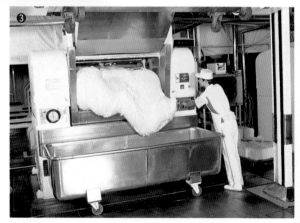

Bakeries, too, are more and more mechanized, computerized, unmanned and automatic.
①**Mixer** Flour is transported from a silo, mixed with water and yeast, then kneaded.
②**Raising Room** Kneaded dough is left to rise 4-5 hours under controlled heat and humidity.
③**Mixer (2nd time)** Flavor is imparted by adding milk, butter, sugar and other ingredients, then dough is kneaded and again left to rise.

Photos:Courtesy of Yamazaki Baking Co., Ltd.

▲ **Sake** A Japanese liquor brewed chiefly from rice, which is mixed with yeast and then fermented.

▲ **Bean Paste** A uniquely Japanese food product. Salt is added to soybeans, rice and other ingredients which are then fermented. Until very recently this type of paste was often made at home.

④ **Oven** Dough-filled steel baking pans are placed in ovens starting at the top. As baking proceeds, they gradually move downward, baking at 230°C for about 30 minutes.

⑤ **Baked Bread** Bread hot from the oven is cooled, then sent to the slicer.

⑥ **Wrapping** After being sliced to the desired thicknesses, bread is wrapped and shipped.

THE TEXTILE INDUSTRY

Textiles as an export developed mainly from the spinning industry. With Korea, China and other emerging industrial countries hot on its heels, and price increases in raw materials sparked by the two oil shocks of the '70s, the industry lost its competitive edge in some items while in others its technological advances, high-grade goods and new products have achieved the world's highest standards.

Raw materials classify the industry into Chemical Fibers (synthetics, rayon, acetate), and Natural Fibers (cotton, wool, silk). Diverse applications of the former range from clothing to industrial uses, with mass-produced synthetics playing a major role in dressing the nation.

The fabric and sewing sectors are mostly small and medium-size concerns. In contrast to the spinning sector, where mechanization has eliminated many jobs, the sewing sector has seen an increase due to the demands from consumers who now can afford fashionable and expensive clothes.

▲**Carbon Fiber in the Space Shuttle Booster** Carbon fiber's lightness and flexibility give it applications ranging from leisure goods to space and aircraft.

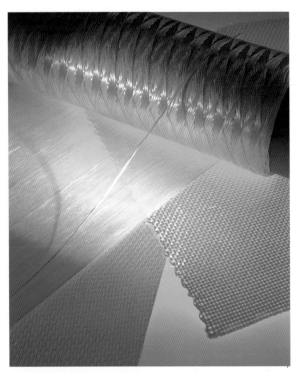

▲**Aluminum Fiber** Another of the new materials. Its properties include high strength, high elasticity and high heat resistance that can strengthen other metals.

▲**Apparel Industry** Its aim is to produce better value-added goods in women's wear, sportswear and other clothing through its materials production.

Photos:Courtesy of Sumitomo Chemical Co., Ltd.

▲(above) **Nylon Spinning** Strong, water-proof, resilient, but poor heat and light resistance. Made along with polyester and acrylic.

▲(above right) **Reeling Raw Silk** The first step in producing silk cloth.

▶(lower right) **Chemical Fiber Mill** Most are small to medium-size firms that process nylon, rayon and other fibers contracted from raw materials makers and traders.

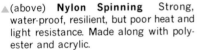

▼**Carding** Removes short fibers.

▼**Combing** Fibers are aligned.

▼**Dyeing** Bobbins are vat-dyed.

▼**Drawing** Stretches, twists fibers.

▼**Weaving** Warp and woof are woven.

▼**Steaming** Strengthens fibers.

PAPER, PULP, AND LUMBER

Japan's paper and cardboard output ranks second to America's, and pulp production stands fourth after the U.S., Canada, and the USSR. Domestically, total shipment value of paper and pulp was 3% of the total value of all industrial production in 1982. Per capita paper consumption went from 27.2kg in 1956 (22nd place) to 46.8kg in 1960 (9th place), with negligible position changes since then.

The three industries consume enormous amounts of resources, so that resource-poor Japan must rely on imports from Canada, the U.S. and others. Chip imports in 1982 ran to 40%.

Japanese houses used to be built mainly of wood and paper, and one by one; but the trend to western-style homes, plus ways to cut construction time and costs, now make prefabrication the usual method. Underlying this are big industry's move into home construction and the American 2 × 4 method. With the spread of the latter, nearly 90% of the wood for new home construction is now dependent on imports.

● Making Paper From Wood Pulp

▲①Chip yard

▶②Chips are chemically treated and steamed to make pulp.

Photos:Courtesy of Oji Paper Co., Ltd.

▲**Wood/Lumber Imports** Despite its reputation for greenery, Japan is deficient in lumber and relies on imports from America, Canada, S. E. Asia and elsewhere.
◀**Home Construction** Lumber, once measured, cut and planed at the jobsite, is nowadays pre-cut at the factory and assembled at the construction site.

▲③Pulp is bleached.

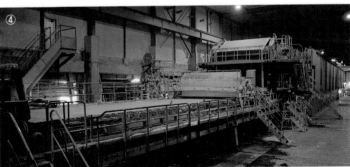

▲④Liquid content is removed, the pulp dried and rolled.

▲⑤Paper sheets are coated.

▲⑥Paper is cut to desired width.

THE STEEL INDUSTRY

Steel is said to be the backbone of Japan's industry. After World War II, under priority measures to increase production, the industry rose from its shattered surroundings and within 30 years grew to a top position in terms of production, equipment and technology. One reason is that directly after the war the industry built large-scale, highly efficient plants at seaside locations, each equipped with state-of-the-art blast furnaces, high output converters, strip mills and central control systems. Another is that the automated forging method gives a rate of production of uniform products that approaches 80%.

Recently, however, not all of this up-to-the-minute equipment has been fully occupied, for domestic demand has become stagnant, protectionist sentiment abroad is heightening, and competition from Korea and other nations is intensifying. To maintain its lead, the industry must try to expand trade through international cooperation, strive to raise productivity by energy conservation and cost control, and endeavor to enhance its products and develop new ones.

▲ Unloading of iron ore and coal, all of which is imported, is done by crane at the ironmill stockyard.

▲ **Rolling Mill Control Room** All operations from unloading of raw materials to shipping out of finished products are computer controlled.

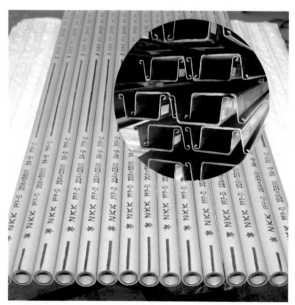

▲ **Steel Products** High-grade even-quality products of steel like these seamless pipes and heavy-duty piles are being produced to meet the needs of the modern era.

● Nonferrous Metals

Major ones include copper, lead, zinc and aluminum. Imports account for most of the raw ore and 100% of the bauxite for aluminum. New metals being developed along with advances in electronics technology include materials that exhibit superconductivity, shape-memory alloys, amorphous and heat-resistant alloys.

▲ **Carbon Fiber** Stronger than steel, light as aluminum. A new materials product with applications ranging from sports equipment to aircraft.

Blast Furnace Operates at 1200-2000°C to turn iron ore, coke and coal into pig iron.

Torpedo Car Transports molten pig iron from the blast furnace to the mill.

Converter Scrap iron is added to pig iron and oxidized to make ingots.

Rolling Metal bars (billets) are reheated and rolled on different machines to fabricate the steel into such items as sheets, pipes, shapes or wire.

Continuous Casting Making steel directly from molten ingots rather than from reheated ones is the present-day method of ensuring products of uniform quality.

Shape-memory Alloy Instantaneously reverts to its original straight shape when heat is applied.

Titanium Roofing Light, strong and highly durable, titanium has wide industrial applications.

SHIPBUILDING

Having lost most of her shipping in World War II, Japan began a planned program of shipbuilding in 1947 that played a major role in the rehabilitation of her merchant fleet. With shipbuilding facilities modernized, the basis was laid for the leap forward which as early as 1956 took the nation past England and made her the world's biggest producer of ships.

The industry is supported by high-tech subcontractors and suppliers. Ships are normally ordered one at a time and built in accordance with their projected use and destination. Firms capable of building ships of over 5000 gross tons number 44, and the industry claims some 200 types of jobs, with 40 different suppliers at the shipyards making 200 products.

The 1973 oil crisis plunged the industry into a slump that saw the yards working at 35% of capacity from 1978 to 1979 and shipbuilding's share of overall exports fell from 10% (1977) to 6% (1983). South Korea and other nations with emerging shipbuilding industries are also taking more and more of the share in international bidding.

▲**Shape Testing**　Models are tested to determine ship shape. Hull construction and sections are designed.

▲**Shakedown Cruise**　The ship undergoes two, and upon success is passed to a captain for its maiden voyage.

▲**Sea-going Oil Rig at the Arctic**　A product of shipbuilding's advanced technology, these rigs are at work in many parts of the world.

▲**Ferryboat**　Japan's many islands and increasingly many cars call for ever larger ferryboats to transport both cars and people.

Block Construction Stern (left) and bow (right) being built in separate docks.

▶ Welding together the two sections of the ship.

▲Outfitting is done at dockside.

▲The ship is launched and taken to sea for trials.

▲**Energy-saving Ship** Equipped with computer-controlled sails to take advantage of wind power and save energy

CONSTRUCTION AND HOUSING INDUSTRIES

Companies in the construction industry range from huge enterprises with high technologies to small specialist firms, all co-existing.

Though the construction industry itself has a long history, the term "housing" is relatively new and includes such facets as sales and construction, land development, mortgages and housing materials.

In the past, house-building was a job for a master carpenter, who in turn hired the needed specialists-plumbers, plasterers, etc. In recent years, however, realtors and the manufacturing sector have made incursions into the field by building large-scale housing complexes and prefabricated units. The result has been the emergence of the industry we now call housing.

Targeted within the next 10 years is the "technopolis", a community of 40-50,000 to be built near population centers of 200-300,000. Each technopolis will comprise high-tech intensive companies, comfortable surroundings for the inhabitants, and universities and research centers.

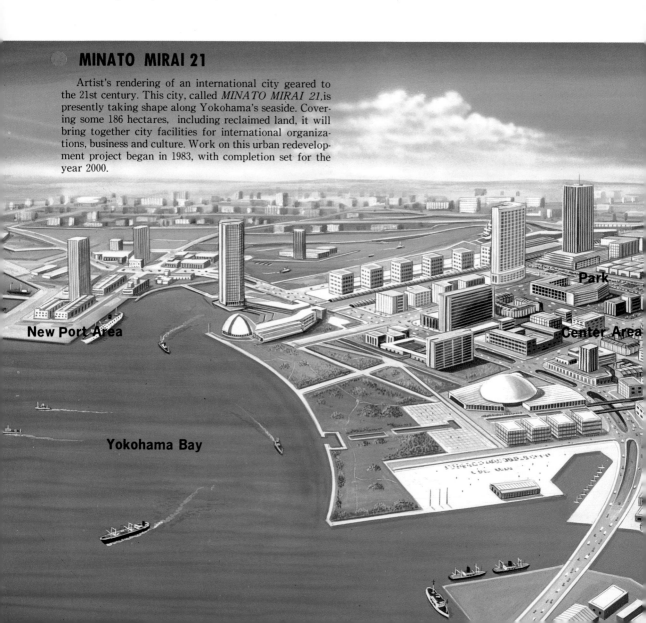

MINATO MIRAI 21

Artist's rendering of an international city geared to the 21st century. This city, called *MINATO MIRAI 21,* is presently taking shape along Yokohama's seaside. Covering some 186 hectares, including reclaimed land, it will bring together city facilities for international organizations, business and culture. Work on this urban redevelopment project began in 1983, with completion set for the year 2000.

New Port Area

Yokohama Bay

Park

Center Area

▲**Onaruto Bridge**   Of the three bridges that eventually will connect the islands of Honshu and Shikoku, this one was begun first (1976) and completed first (1985).

▶ Apartment complexes like this one in Kobe are increasingly common around metropolitan areas.

▲**Modular Type Home of New Ceramics**   Produced at the factory, assembled at the site. Requires only two weeks for completion, including foundation work.

▼**Environmental Test Chamber**   Recreates heavy snows, blizzards and other conditions for all-weather testing.

ENERGY

Japan's energy-supply policy was, from the '50s, one that put dependence on oil; but the jump in crude prices after the first oil shock and a need for reserves gave pause to that policy. With energy conservation now the basis, there has been a shift in recent years toward more reliance on nuclear power, LNG, coal and other non-oil sources, plus development of solar energy and coal liquefaction.

Japan's energy consumption is low among the advanced nations. Calculated in oil, annual per capita is 2336 kg—only 37% of that for America, 36% for Canada, and 77% of that for England. It is, however, rising yearly. In terms of oil it was 388 million kl in 1982, with projections of 460 million for 1990 and 530 for 1995.

Research in nuclear power use began in the late 1950s. By 1981, 23 plants were in operation, generating 16% of total power output. This went to 20% in 1983, so that nuclear power is increasingly replacing oil as the mainstay in generation.

Solar energy use is also being actively pursued. Solar cells, solar homes and solar power generators are already at the point where they are beginning to be widespread.

Atomic Power Plant at Fukushima
Most power in Japan is thermal, though nuclear plants are in all parts of the nation and their use is on the increase.

Geothermal Plant at Naruko
Underground steam and hot water generate about one million kw.

Wind Power Station at Kagoshima
Still in the testing stage but is Japan's largest, capable of 300 kw.

Photos:Courtesy of Mitsubishi Electric Corporation & Sumitomo Electric Industries, Ltd.

▲**Solar Cell System in Okinawa** Transforms sunlight directly into electrical power. Especially useful for offshore islands. Auxilliary generator ensures a stable supply of power on inclement days.

▲**Solar House** Uses solar energy for heating, cooling and other purposes. Many homes are equipped with smaller versions for energy conservation.

▲**Super-conductive Magnet** World's largest energy stockpiler. Used in nuclear fusion apparatus, the study of matter, energy stockpiling.

▲**Oil Depot** Japan's energy base is mainly oil-dependent. Some 98% of needed oil comes from abroad by super tanker and is stored at depots.

DISTRIBUTION DIVERSIFICATION

Propelled by the high growth of the late 1950s, industry surged ahead, factories turned out masses of goods, per-capita income rose and, with the population moving into the cities, mass consumption followed, bringing various changes in the flow of goods from maker to consumer.

On the retail level, supermarkets played a leading role. They effected savings by volume-buying and self-service, lowered prices and grew big in the process.

To move masses of goods efficiently meant more and larger trucks, highways, super tankers, container ships and automated cargo-handling, plus distribution centers in large cities. Increasingly, such centers are computerized to cope with the inflow and outflow of shipments.

▲**Freeways** As truck transport makes greater and greater headway there is a corresponding need for an expanded network of freeways. Photo shows the Suita Interchange on the Meishin Freeway.

▶**Detergent Shipment and Control Room for Computer-aided Dispatching** Type and quantity of detergent is automatically issued from warehouse on commands from computer. Monitors above terminal show warehouse interior.

Photos:Courtesy of Kao Soap Co., Ltd. & Japan Air Lines Co., Ltd.

▲**Truck Delivery**   Trucks are constantly on the move between producers and delivery terminals, outstripping rails as carriers of goods and offering next-day delivery.

▲**Distribution Center (Tokyo)**   Grouping of delivery depots, truck terminals and warehouses for computer-aided storage and shipment of goods.

▲**Truck Terminal (Tokyo)**   Long-haul carriers and short-haul city trucks transfer freight or deposit it for short-term storage. Mainly built in traffic-congested large cities.

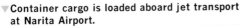

▼**Container cargo is loaded aboard jet transport at Narita Airport.**

▼**Container Pier (Kobe)**   Transfer, loading and unloading, and storage of containers and freight are mostly automated.

SUPERMARKETS AND DEPARTMENT STORES

Until just recently, department stores enjoyed a solid and influential position in the retail field. With the advent of the supermarket, however, their power and sweep are undergoing changes.

The line between department store and supermarket is hard to draw. One definition is that a store with sales space of at least 100m², 50% or more of which is for self-service, is a supermarket.

Since their first appearance they have spread rapidly. Annual sales in 1972 by-passed those for department stores, and doubled them in 1979. Low consumer spending in recent years has intensified competition between them, and both sponsor a variety of attractions to entice buyers. Exhibitions, galleries, playlands for children, as well as delivery and automated playguide services are but a few of the promotion policies of department stores, whereas supermarkets have altered their style and now include 24-hour service and discount shops.

▲**Art Gallery at a Department Store** Almost everything under the sun is available at Japan's department stores. Some even feature their own art galleries.

▲**Rooftop Playland** Many department stores provide small-scale amusement parks on their roofs to please the youngsters and attract customers.

● THE DISTRIBUTION OF GOODS

The distribution system in Japan is highly complex. Dealers' infrastructures differ according to the type of merchandise handled, and wholesalers are divided and subdivided into various tiers, with still other middlemen at the area of production.

Such a complicated network makes for higher expenses so that a substantial difference emerges between the producer's price and that paid by the consumer. Movements to simplify the flow of goods and lower their prices have intensified, as in streamlining the supermarket route or in the emergence of stores purchasing directly from the producing localities.

● **Banana Distribution And Price Changes**

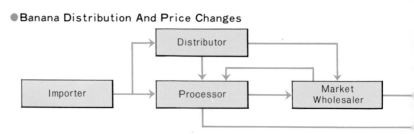

● **White Shirt Distribution And Price Changes**

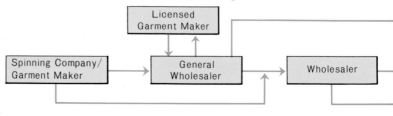

Photos:Courtesy of Sogo Stores, Ltd.

◀▲**Ginza Area Department Store**   Within a radius of only 300 meters there are eight department stores vying for customers.

▲**Convenience Store**   Many are open 24 hours a day, attracting shift-workers, nightowls and the young.

▲**Supermarket Parking Lot**   Suburban supermarkets provide ample parking for their customers.

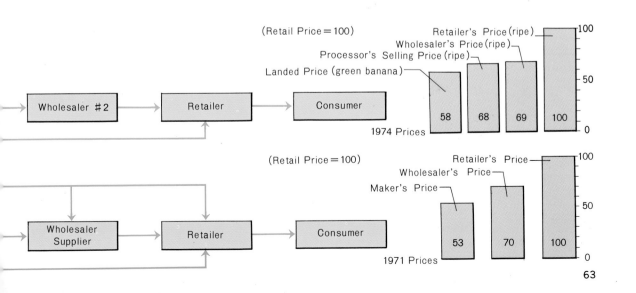

(Retail Price = 100)

Retailer's Price (ripe)
Wholesaler's Price (ripe)
Processor's Selling Price (ripe)
Landed Price (green banana)

| Wholesaler #2 | → | Retailer | → | Consumer |

58   68   69   100

100

50

0

1974 Prices

(Retail Price = 100)

Retailer's Price
Wholesaler's Price
Maker's Price

| Wholesaler Supplier | | Retailer | → | Consumer |

53   70   100

100

50

0

1971 Prices

SPECIALTY SHOPS

As life becomes more affluent, consumer wants become more varied, and shops specializing in a single line with a large assortment now attract many customers. There are also areas such as Akihabara in Tokyo, and Nihonbashi in Osaka, where entire streets are given over to shops dealing only in electric and electronic goods and parts. In addition to these two main outlets for such items, a similar one exists in Tokyo's Shinjuku area for cameras. These clusters of shops in the same field increase the range of goods, and make it hard for a customer not to find what he or she is looking for. Groupings such as these also invite competition, better service and lower prices.

Specialty shops are also ones like boutiques or stores that carry clothing and accessory items, all expressing one particular mode. They may also be large-volume operations such as the camera stores in Shinjuku that also offer items outside the camera field such as watches and audiovisual equipment.

▲ **Electrical Goods Shop in Akihabara** Such shops have proliferated to the extent that they now form whole avenues known for selling almost anything in the electrical/electronics field at low prices.

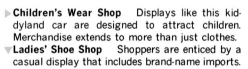

▲**Do-It-Yourself Store** Ubiquitous in both town and suburbs, they provide most anything in wood, metal or leather, as well as instruction and classes.

▲**Camera Shop in Shinjuku** Selling cameras, watches, calculators and other maker-direct items, such shops crowd the area and oftentimes cut prices more than 50%.

▶**Children's Wear Shop** Displays like this kiddyland car are designed to attract children. Merchandise extends to more than just clothes.

▼**Ladies' Shoe Shop** Shoppers are enticed by a casual display that includes brand-name imports.

THE SHINKANSEN(BULLET TRAIN)AND THE TRANSPORTATION NETWORK

Japan has an excellent transportation network, in particular its Shinkansen. Fast (maximum speed: 210 km/hour), safe, and always on time, it has had no accidents resulting in injury or death since it began service in 1964.

On the Tokyo-Osaka run, a train leaves each station every 15 minutes during the rush hours and invariably arrives on time. Each day some 440,000 passengers ride the Shinkansen.

The latest in electronic technology is used to run the trains efficiently and safely: the ATC (Automatic Train Control) and the CTC (Centralized Train Control). The ATC regulates train speed, running them at minimum intervals of 3 km and slowing them to a pre-set speed when encountering curves.

The CTC monitors all moving trains, and displays their numbers, positions, signals from the ATC and wind velocity along the tracks.

In large cities like Tokyo and Osaka, the transportation network of trains, buses and subways is complex to the point that even the inhabitants have difficulty trying to understand it.

▲ **Tokaido Shinkansen** Trains run every 15 minutes, forming an indispensable mode of transport for business people, tourists and other passengers.

▶ **Shinkansen Central Control** The movements of all trains underway can be monitored at a glance and controlled for safety and time schedules.

▲**Linear Motor Car** Hailed as the next-generation mode of transport, the LMC has tested out at a top speed of 519km/hour and is only a step away from actual use.

▲**Demand Bus** A compact bus designed to run on narrow city streets. Bus stops are equipped with a sensor that displays bus movements. Passengers can alight at points other than bus stops upon "demand" (=pressing the button) and have a choice of cash, tokens or plastic cards.

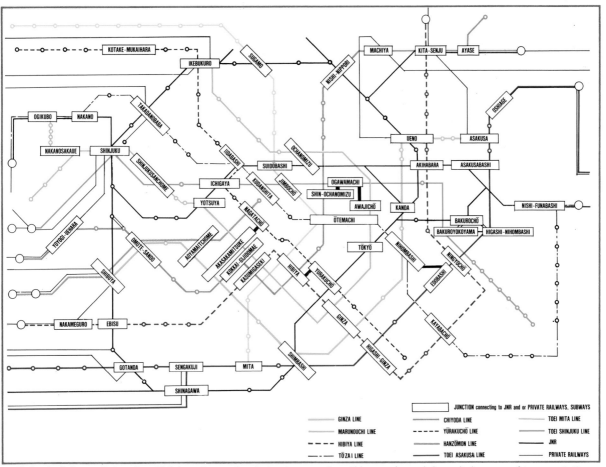

Tokyo's Subway Network Oblivious to overhead street congestion, this complex web is a vital means of transportation for millions every day.

THE INFORMATION INDUSTRY

Japan's publishing industry is presently in a slump: sales are slow but new publications continue to increase. Books alone ran to 29,300 new titles in 1981, leaping to 33,600 in 1984 so that competition for space in already crowded bookstores is intense. Turnover, too, has speeded up, with magazine display time three days and new publications one week. The return rate until around 1971 was 30%, exceeded 35% in 1981, and reached some 40% in 1984, leading to fierce competition by publishers and excessive shipments by distributors. Only comics show any improvement.

With book publishing in a slump, interest is now on such computer-aided new media as video disc books and CD-ROM works. CAPTAIN, CATV and other systems are operating, as are LAN and VAN. Computers and computer-related equipment in the information industry are expanding 15-20% yearly.

▲**Part-time Work Information Via On-Line** Display panels can be found at train stations and bookstores. Information on desired part-time work is available for a mere ¥10.

▲**E-DRAW (Erasable-Direct Read After Write)** Large amounts of information can be recorded on optical format discs, replayed and erased. Interest is centering on their use as a new mode for information files.

▲**Laser-vision Disc Production** LVDs—records that produce pictures—are drawing interest as a new media for sports, hobbies and cultural enrichment.

▲**Subscriber Data Transmission Via CATV Network** The development of CATV promises diverse and personalized information and entertainment.

 Photos:Courtesy of Pioneer Electric Corporation & GAKKEN MEDICON.

Book Center The entire building is a huge book store, with most domestic publications in stock. Inset shows area around entrance. (Tokyo Station, Yaesu Book Center)

City Information Via Laser Disc Terminals are set up in the busier parts of town to provide information on entertainment, dining, drinking and other leisure activities.

CAPTAIN System This information service is available at banks, hotels and other locations, and is beginning to spread to homes.

THE LEISURE INDUSTRY

A boom in such leisure activities as Sunday driving, bowling and trips abroad led to a leisure-market surge around 1965. That, and increased leisure time due to shortened workhours and the spread of the two-day weekend gave the leisure industry a high growth, which, despite set-backs in the economy from the oil shock and low consumer spending, has not changed, for the demand for leisure remains unabated.

Small-scale pursuits enjoyed close to home, and larger-scale ones like trips abroad, are the two divisions of leisure. In the former, Japanese chess, *Go,* and mahjong have long been popular, with do-it-yourself (weekend carpentry, etc.) and gardening gaining new appreciation. Japan has some 5 million anglers, and golf and tennis have gained many enthusiasts in recent years. Noticeable, too, is the recent rise in health, athletic and swimming clubs for physical fitness. Despite stiff membership fees, they are thriving, as are trips overseas, with some 4% of the population abroad in 1984.

Sightseeing Trips and drives hold top spots as ways to enjoy time off. Sightseeing areas abound in Japan, with Kyoto, Nara, and Nikko especially popular, so that shrines, temples, souvenir shops and hotels bustle with throngs of family groups, young singles, students on school trips and many visitors from abroad.

▲ **Kyoto**   **Heian Shrine**
▶ **Kyoto**   **Approach to Sanzen-in**

▲ **Tokyo Disneyland**   Opened in 1983, this park, like the original in California, attracts some 10 million tourists annually.

▲ **Safari Park**   Such parks, where animals can be viewed in realistic surroundings, have become popular destinations for family outings.

▲ **Golf Course**   Over 1200 golf courses dot Japan's limited land area. Weekends are so crowded that reservations are necessary to insure a chance on the green.

▲ **Athletic Club**   Membership fees are high at private clubs that feature facilities for swimming, dancing and athletic activities.

▲ **Overseas Travel**   With trips abroad undergoing a boom, especially among young women, Japan's international airports are congested during vacation periods.

▲ **Kabuki Theater**   Light and easy forms of leisure activities include movies and theater-going. Among middle-aged women, kabuki is highly popular.

THE RESTAURANT INDUSTRY

Japanese eating habits have undergone a big change in the last 20 years. The average family nowadays eats a breakfast based on bread rather than rice, and enjoys western, Chinese, and European style foods for the other daily meals as well.

Eating out has also seen big changes under a more affluent life-style. With rice no longer the staple, personal preference plays a bigger role in food choice. The increase in working women and working couples also means more opportunities for not eating at home, as does the spread of the two-day weekend.

Japan has some 800,000 eating and drinking establishments, 20% of which offer Japanese, Chinese or western-style menus, a diversity that underscores Japan's reputation as a nation with international tastes. Many such restaurants are at department stores, where a common scene has the father eating Chinese food, the mother a French dish, the children Italian-style spaghetti and the grandparents enjoying a Japanese meal, all at the same table.

Not much capital is needed to open a restaurant, but the trend nowadays is away from this due to American chains like McDonald's or Denny's and Japanese fast-food or family restaurant chains, all of which are sprouting everywhere and require huge outlays.

▲**Family Restaurant** Inexpensive and offering good service, these big-venture chains are a hit with families. In some areas there are clusters of these American-style restaurants, and their popularity among the young is reflected in the long lines of cars on weekends.

▲**Department Store Restaurant** Types of food available include Japanese, western and Chinese, usually with plastic models in outside display windows.

▲**Coffee Shop** Coffee shops in Japan offer coffee, soft drinks and light orders in a subdued atmosphere that makes them ideal for dates, business, coffee breaks.

▲**Take-out Orders** Service of this kind has long been practiced by sushi bars, noodle shops and other eating establishments, with free delivery to the customer's door.

▲**Tavern** At the end of the workday the businessman often heads for his favorite among these drinking establishments to enjoy sake, beer or whatever his thirst demands.

▲**Fast Food Restaurant** Many are foreign franchises. Their informality and convenience have made them almost ubiquitous around the nation.

AGRICULTURE

Rice production is at the core of agriculture in Japan. By dint of hard work, farmers have long obtained high yields from limited arable land and have developed it more fully through soil improvement, plant breeding and technology.

Such methods, plus the development of cold-resistant seeds, gave rise to the rapid growth in rice production in northern Japan after World War II.

Since the latter half of the 1950s, farm mechanization, pesticides and herbicides have rapidly spread, greatly reducing labor. However, the increasing costs of mechanization have strained finances to the extent that full-time farmers have dropped to fewer than 600,000 at present. The self-sufficiency rate in staple grains has also fallen: it was 60% in 1980.

Biotechnological research in agriculture is currently underway in such wide-ranging areas as DNA replacement for improved plant breeding, and the cultivation of superior strains through cloning.

▲**Small Land-plots**　Small paddies march right up steep hillsides as farmers strive to utilize every speck of arable land.

▲**Part-time Farmers**　More and more farming is being left to wives and the old folks as heads of households leave the homestead to seek work elsewhere.

 Photos : Courtesy of Kyowa Hakko Kogyo Co., Ltd & Mitsubishi Electric Corporation.

▲**Forced vegetables**   Lettuce and other leafy vegetables are cultivated indoors using artificial methods that yield crops quickly regardless of the season.

◀Biotechnology can take one bulb and, over the space of a year, make it yield trillions. Through such techniques, new plant varieties can be massproduced in a short time.

▲**Vegetable Growth Experiment**   Various experiments are undertaken for strain improvement and hastened growth.

▲**Hot-house Culturing**   Cucumbers, tomatoes, bell peppers and other vegetables are cultivated indoors with no regard to the seasons.

THE FORESTRY INDUSTRY

Japan is a nation rich in mountains and forests, but with its small land area, only 25,000,000 hectares are wooded, a negligible figure when compared with that for the U.S., the USSR and others. Japan also suffers from a perpetual insufficiency in wood, attributable to the war-time use of most of it as fuel and lumber, the delay in recovery, and the fact that post-war new growth cannot yet be fully used.

Annual lumber consumption comes to some 65,730,000m³. Half is imported, mainly from America, the USSR and Malaysia, who supply 75%. Most of the imports used to be logs, but this has now shifted to processed lumber in line with the conservation policies of exporting nations and the trend to export finished, value-added materials.

Some 81% of present-day total demand is for processed lumber or plywood. The spread of prefabrication and the 2 × 4 method have expanded the demand for plywood, so that imports from the U.S. and Indonesia have accelerated, leaving Japanese plywood makers in a slump.

▶ **Cedar Woods** The Japanese prize cedar as a building material and for woodwork. Three forests (one each in Akita, Kyoto and Shikoku) are called Japan's Three Beauties. Photo: cedar forest in Akita.

● AFORESTATION

①**Seedlings** Seeds planted in a field grow into seedlings in 3-4 years.
②**Transplanting** Seedlings are dug up and taken to the mountains to be planted.
③**Clearing** For 5-8 years after trees are planted, weeds that might interfere with growth are cleared away one or two times a year.
④**Thinning** Trees that show little promise of surviving and random growth are cut down.
  Intermittent Thinning Starting with the 15th year and for a number of years thereafter, trees are thinned out to eliminate weak and dead ones and allow more space and sunlight, leaving about one in four.
⑤**Pruning** Excess lower limbs are sawn off after about the 15th year to prevent gnarls, protect against insects and promote straight growth.

④

⑤

▼**Snow-damaged Trees (Fukushima Prefecture)** Heavy snows in 1981 caused much tree damage in eastern Japan. Many forests have also suffered from typhoons and high winds.

THE FISHING INDUSTRY

Japan, surrounded by water, is known as a fishing and a fish-consuming nation, with coastal, off-shore and deep-sea fishing industries.

Expansion of coastal operations has been made difficult due to overfishing, pollution and other problems, but off-shore and deep-sea catches have had annual increases, with the latter accounting for 40% of the total catch in 1970. More nations, however, are observing the 200-mile zone, so that Japan's deep-sea catches have dropped. Off-shore ones, however, have risen, due to technological advances and have, since 1978, accounted for over 50% of the total catch.

Since deep-sea fishing is expected to become even more restricted, the Japanese industry must develop its coastal and off-shore fishing, turn processing into a more profitable industry, and shift from catching fish to farming them.

In fact, aquaculture, since 1980, has supplied over 20% of the total catch, due to biotechnological advances and new developments in breeding techniques.

▲**Seafood Processing Plant**　Japan is known worldwide as a fishing nation as well as a processor of canned fish and fish paste.

▲**Dried Bonito**　The fish is treated with a special mold, then allowed to dry and harden. Its rich flavor is highly appreciated as a base for other foods.

▲**Fish Market**　Catches and marine products from around the world are auctioned every morning to start the flow of products from wholesalers to retailers.

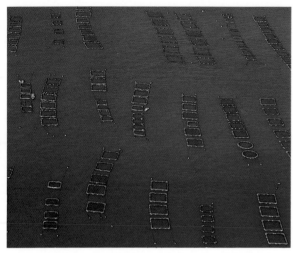

▲**Pearl Culture**   Implanting a shell nucleus into an akoya oyster then suspending it from a raft (photo) will yield a lustrous pearl in about four years.

▲**Bluefin Culture**   Farming of bluefin, flatfish, lobster, seabream and other high-grade fish is active. Bio-tech aids such as artificial incubation are employed.

●SALMON HATCHERY

▲Adult salmon return to spawn and are caught.

▲Eggs are removed from the female abdomen.

▲Sperm from the male fertilizes the eggs.

▲Eggs are incubated in running water at 8°C.

In autumn, salmon return to the rivers where they were born in order to spawn. They are caught and their eggs removed, artificially fertilized and incubated. The young fish are raised until they are 4-5 cm long, then released into rivers and head for the sea. After 3-4 years the full-grown salmon return and are caught. In recent years, thanks to advances in releasing methods and other techniques, the annual catch has risen to as many as 30 million, almost topping the salmon and trout catches made in northern waters.

▲Eyes appear some 30 days after fertilization. Hatching occurs about 60 days later.

▼Fully grown salmon (60-90cm long) are caught when they head back to the rivers of their origin.

▼Young fish are fed in captivity 1-2 months until 4-5 cm long, then released.

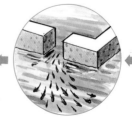

WORLD TRADE

Japan's trade, like that of England and a number of West European nations, is often referred to by the term "processing trade," meaning imported raw materials, exported finished goods.

Japan's trade and economy expanded rapidly from around 1955. Exports, once mainly in textiles, other light industries and heavy chemicals, are now chiefly in precision machine industries, cars, home electronics and other knowledge-intensive industries. Imports have changed too, with fewer in raw fibers, more in LPG, LNG and other fossil fuels.

Trading partners include America, the many nations ringing the Pacific basin, and most other nations of the world.

Ideally, trade among nations should be balanced, but recently Japan's exports have exceeded imports to the extent that its trade partners, under a surfeit of them, are moving to limit or restrict them. That and other factors have given rise to trade friction. For Japan, trade is its life-blood, making it essential to develop more trade and reduce trade friction.

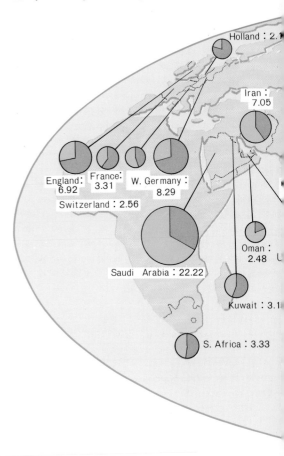

Holland : 2.
Iran : 7.05
England : 6.92
France: 3.31
W. Germany : 8.29
Switzerland : 2.56
Oman : 2.48
Saudi Arabia : 22.22
Kuwait : 3.1
S. Africa : 3.33

■Japan's Major Exports: Destinations and Amounts

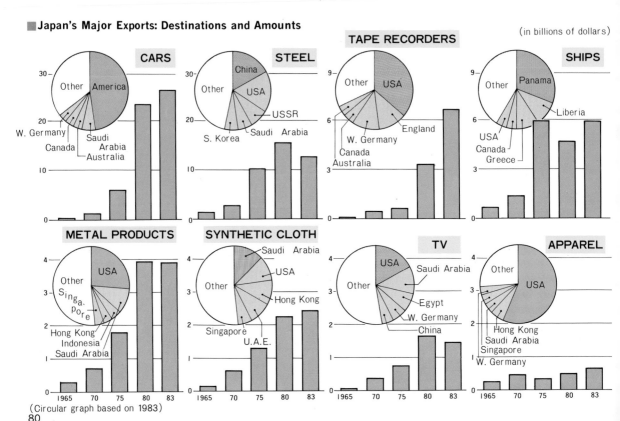

(in billions of dollars)

CARS
30 —
Other | America
20 —
W. Germany
Canada | Saudi Arabia
Australia
10 —
0 —

STEEL
30 —
China
Other | USA
20 —
USSR
S. Korea | Saudi Arabia
10 —
0 —

TAPE RECORDERS
9 —
Other | USA
England
W. Germany
Canada
Australia
6 —
3 —
0 —

SHIPS
9 —
Other | Panama
Liberia
USA
Canada
Greece
6 —
3 —
0 —

METAL PRODUCTS
4 —
Other | USA
Singapore
3 —
Hong Kong
Indonesia
Saudi Arabia
2 —
1 —
0 —
1965 70 75 80 83

SYNTHETIC CLOTH
4 —
Saudi Arabia
USA
Other
Hong Kong
3 —
Singapore
U.A.E.
2 —
1 —
0 —
1965 70 75 80 83

TV
4 —
USA | Saudi Arabia
Other
Egypt
W. Germany
China
3 —
2 —
1 —
0 —
1965 70 75 80 83

APPAREL
4 —
Other
USA
3 —
Hong Kong
Saudi Arabia
Singapore
W. Germany
2 —
1 —
0 —
1965 70 75 80 83

(Circular graph based on 1983)

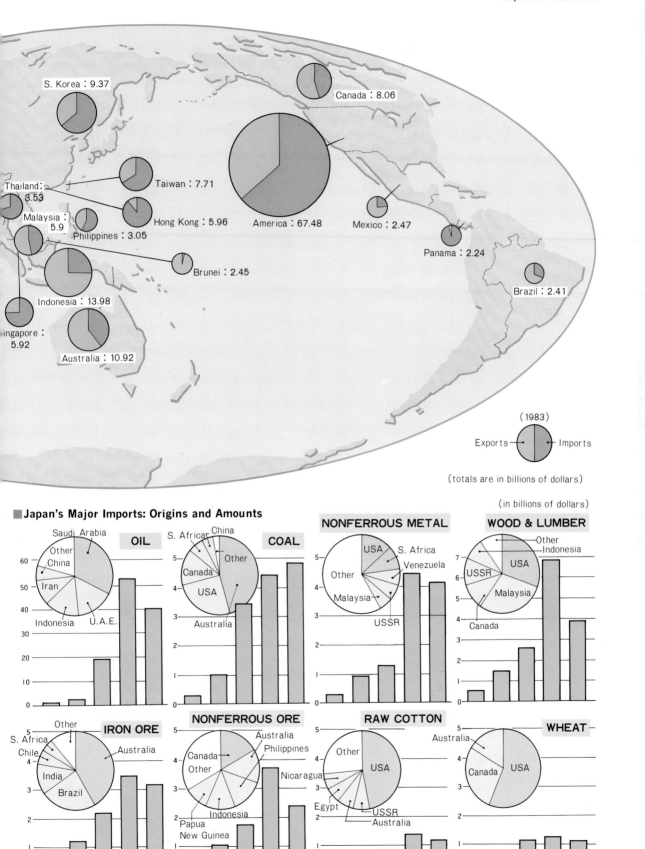

S. Korea : 9.37

Canada : 8.06

Thailand :
3.53

Taiwan : 7.71

Malaysia :
5.9

Hong Kong : 5.96

America : 67.48

Mexico : 2.47

Philippines : 3.05

Brunei : 2.45

Panama : 2.24

Indonesia : 13.98

Brazil : 2.41

ingapore :
5.92

Australia : 10.92

(1983)

Exports ― ― Imports

(totals are in billions of dollars)

(in billions of dollars)

■Japan's Major Imports: Origins and Amounts

OIL

Saudi Arabia
Other
China
Iran
Indonesia
U.A.E.

COAL

S. African
China
Other
Canada
USA
Australia

NONFERROUS METAL

USA
S. Africa
Venezuela
Other
Malaysia
USSR

WOOD & LUMBER

Other
Indonesia
USSR
USA
Malaysia
Canada

IRON ORE

Other
S. Africa
Chile
India
Brazil
Australia

NONFERROUS ORE

Australia
Philippines
Canada
Other
Nicaragua
Indonesia
Papua
New Guinea

RAW COTTON

Australia
Other
USA
Egypt
USSR
Australia

WHEAT

Australia
Canada
USA

1965 70 75 80 83

(Circular graphs based on 1983)

81

JAPANESE-STYLE MANAGEMENT

In general, employment at a Japanese company is from date of hire to day of retirement. Salary and position depend on age and seniority rather than ability and performance, although ability pay has lately been introduced and both systems are in use.

The employer-employee relationship is not confined to what transpires at the workplace, for great importance is put on a close inter-personal bond. Company recreation days and outings, trips, parties, a company song and uniform are all common and help to strengthen the company tie and inspire work.

▲**Uniform**　To strengthen the sense of oneness with the company, many firms require the wearing of uniforms.

▲**Company Recreation Day**　With family members also taking part, the emotional tie to the company is deepened.

▲**Morning Assembly**　Prior to the start of the workday, everyone assembles, exchanges greetings, hears a pep talk and the day's agenda as a way of generating a working spirit.

▲**Seals**　These carry more weight in Japanese business than do signatures in other nations. Documents often bear a number of seals from the company president on down. Signatures, too, are starting to be used.

THE EVERYDAY LIFE OF THE JAPANESE

JAPANESE HOUSES

Around 1950, houses were scarce; but in the '60s the influx of people into the cities and the need for housing for the post-war baby boomers set the home construction industry into motion. So many housing developments, apartment complexes and high-rise condominiums were built that the slogan "One Family-One Dwelling" became a reality.

Standards, however, were low enough to have led one EC official to liken Japanese houses to rabbit hutches. Owner sophistication, too, showed itself in complaints about size, construction and surroundings, and in desires for improved quality.

Destruction of the natural environment for housing developments has also raised concern. The lack of space in big cities also means a long commute to the workplace, and house lots of less than 100m² are now a commonplace.

Japanese houses were once built of wood due to its abundance and suitability to the climate, but now, because of the westernization of Japan's life-style and changes in construction methods, they come in a variety of styles and mixtures.

▲**High-Rise Housing Complex** These large-scale housing areas are home to thousands and often have their own schools, parks, markets and other facilities. Many residents commute to work in the big cities.

▼**Condominium** Living units like these connote an image of class and are accordingly referred to in Japanese by the word *manshon.* Their proximity to downtown areas and easy maintenance outweigh their small size.

● Home Floorspace

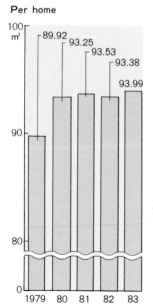

Per home

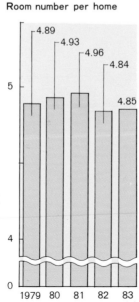

Room number per home

▲**Old-fashioned Residential Area** These old-style wooden homes in Kyoto evoke the atmosphere of a bygone era.

▼**New Housing Area** New towns like this are appearing on the outskirts of cities where hills and fields used to stand.

●PRIVATE HOMES

Old homes that retain some of the traditional architectural style once followed by farmers, merchants, tradesmen and lower echelon *samurai* are called *minka*. Some are said to be over 300 years old. The sturdy wooden framework is a product of a bygone era.

▼**Exterior of an Old Private Home**

▲**Living Room** Thick wooden pillars support a large, heavy roof. The hearth in the center functioned as a family gathering place.

FAMILIES AND HOMES

Until recently, the extended family held sway in Japan, so that households averaged five persons. Now, with emphasis on the nuclear family, there are three to four. Many young couples live apart from their in-laws while the latter enjoy good health, a trend seen especially in cities.

Japanese houses were once designed to accommodate guests, but with the nuclear family at the forefront, emphasis in home construction is now on family life. The parlor—once the center of the home—has given way to the living or dining area, and the kitchen brought out of the closet to become a bright and clean family-centered area. Hinged doors have replaced sliding ones, separate bedrooms and children's rooms allow for privacy, while western-style rooms and bathrooms with modern fixtures have also increased, as have new home-construction materials.

In Japan's hot and humid summer, houses of wood had the advantage of coolness. *Tatami, shoji*, and *fusuma* (partitions) are other climatic adaptations and should not be allowed to disappear under the westernization of life. It is unfortunate, indeed, that other architectural features (the decorative alcove, Buddhist altar, veranda, etc.) are fast passing from the scene.

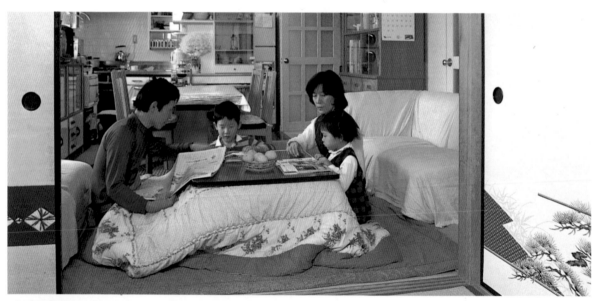

▲**Living Room**   The Japanese *kotatsu* (footwarmer) and sitting on the floor are two aspects of the Japanese life-style that remain unchanged despite the chairs, tables, sofas, carpets and other western-style furniture.

▲**Garden**   Some are so small that they are jokingly referred to as a cat's forehead. Even so, plants are planted and carefully tended.

● **Typical Floorplan**

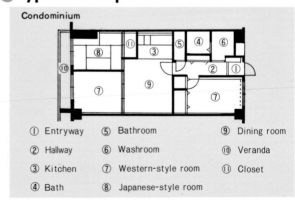

Condominium

① Entryway	⑤ Bathroom	⑨ Dining room
② Hallway	⑥ Washroom	⑩ Veranda
③ Kitchen	⑦ Western-style room	⑪ Closet
④ Bath	⑧ Japanese-style room	

▲Entryway This is where one changes from shoes to slippers upon entering a house. Since guests are also greeted here, it is decorated and given much care.

▲Veranda A uniquely Japanese adjunct to a room with a good southern exposure. It is here, as opposed to the entryway, that close friends are received. As an architectural feature it is fast disappearing.

▲Parlor Easily the nicest room in the house—and the most expensive to build. Mainly for guests and various ceremonies, though few homes nowadays have a parlor.

▲The Bath The tub is for warming and relaxing the body, which is washed before getting in. Such clean use of the water allows the entire family to use it in turn.

▶Bathroom Although western fixtures are now common, there are still many flush-type Japanese ones.

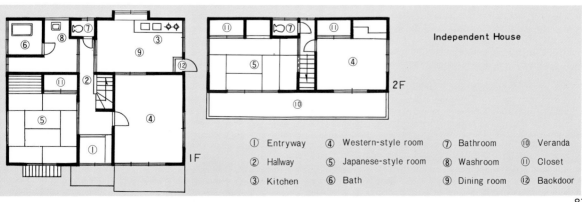

Independent House

2F

1F

① Entryway	④ Western-style room	⑦ Bathroom	⑩ Veranda
② Hallway	⑤ Japanese-style room	⑧ Washroom	⑪ Closet
③ Kitchen	⑥ Bath	⑨ Dining room	⑫ Backdoor

FAMILIES AND EXPENSES

After the slump of 1980–83, the economy began to pick up, with consumer prices comparatively stable. Household income, however, remains tight, spending is slow, and an ever higher share of family income derives from working wives.

Outlays for food, rent, utilities, clothing and miscellaneous items consume some 90% of real income–high when compared to other advanced nations. More is being spent on entertainment, recreation and education, with those in their 40s making especially heavy outlays for housing and children's education.

Purchases of cars, VCRs, personal computers and other durable goods occupy a widening share of expenditures, although maker-competition curbs prices.

The personal-savings rate (bank deposits, insurance, securities or other forms) is higher than in many other nations. Reasons include inadequate social security, time-plan savings for major purchases, and providing for emergencies.

In a recent public opinion poll that asked what class of society one belonged to, 90% checked the box marked "Middle", and many, especially those in the 30-49 age group, checked the box that said, "Life is hard."

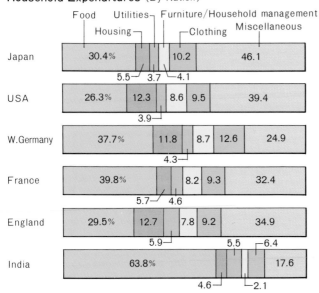

Household Expenditures (By Nation)

	Food	Housing	Utilities	Furniture/Household management	Clothing	Miscellaneous
Japan	30.4%	5.5	3.7	4.1	10.2	46.1
USA	26.3%	12.3	3.9	8.6	9.5	39.4
W.Germany	37.7%	11.8	4.3	8.7	12.6	24.9
France	39.8%	5.7	4.6	8.2	9.3	32.4
England	29.5%	12.7	5.9	7.8	9.2	34.9
India	63.8%		4.6	5.5	2.1	17.6

Rate Of Durable Goods Ownership (In Japan)

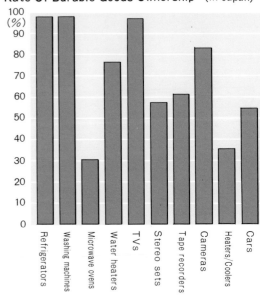

Refrigerators, Washing machines, Microwave ovens, Water heaters, TVs, Stereo sets, Tape recorders, Cameras, Heaters/Coolers, Cars

▲**Bank**   The Japanese are great savers, putting anything over the average annual income into a variety of savings institutions.

▲**University Students** Expenses for education have now topped 20% of household expenditures.

◀**Grape Gathering**   Many families enjoy going out in the family car to pick whatever fruit is in season as a good way to beat the ever-increasing costs of leisure activities.

▲**Kitchen** Ovens, refrigerators, freezers and other durable consumer goods are now a commonplace and have considerably lightened household labor.

▲**Housing**   Land and houses are expensive. Prices now average 10 times annual income and monthly payments put a heavy strain on household finances.

THE BUSINESSMAN AT WORK

When something is to be decided in a Japanese company, the first step is to hold a meeting, through which goals are defined, opinions unified, responsibility shared and morale heightened.

Upon employment at a company, the usual practice is to work there until retirement. For the employee, then, life at the company and the relationships built there are of the utmost importance. To aid the way, firms lay out huge sums for company recreation days, culture festivals, trips and year-end parties. In-house papers and occasional addresses by the president are also usual practices to help raise and maintain a working spirit. At many companies, the day begins with calisthenics for everyone, followed by a morning meeting to set the day's goals.

In mid-summer and at year's end gifts are customarily given to those who have been of help. This makes a good impression and furthers mutual trust and relationships.

A big problem nowadays for some older businessmen is how to cope with the influx of OA equipment making its way into the office. Many disdain both it and the computer, whereas for the younger people adjustment is swift. A further problem is that while the older generation has been company-centered, the younger is inclined to put individual work first.

▲**Conference** In Japanese business practices there is a conference for everything. Opinions are unified and importance placed on teamwork.

▶**Workplace OA** The '80s have seen a sudden surge in office automation, making mastery of it a duty and giving rise to the term "computer allergy."

●IN-COMPANY TRAINING

Company training is carried out to foster a company spirit and thoroughly indoctrinate employees into company policies. There are, among others, orientation programs for new employees, and skills and spiritual training.

For the first few months, new employees are lodged together, given orientation tours, and thoroughly taught what they need to know about management policies and the right company atmosphere.

For middle-management there is also spiritual and psychological training, which usually takes the form of a grueling schedule of Zen meditation at temples, role-play in mock conferences and other methods to bring out and develop abilities as managers.

▶ **Language Training** English conversation is a must for the businessman, and many firms hire native-speaker instructors to teach it.

▲**Morning Calisthenics** At many companies employees engage in light calisthenics prior to the day's start, limbering up the body and enhancing the will to work.

▲**Overtime** Work comes first for the businessman, who at busy times must burn the midnight oil and even go to the office on Sundays and other days off.

▼**Addresses** Many lectures on management policy and ideas are given to employees by those higher up the corporate ladder to cultivate the sense of unity with the company and promote a high morale.

▼**Entertaining** Business agreements are often concluded by entertaining at expensive restaurants or invitations to golf. Trust and personal relationships figure more highly than clauses in a contract when making business deals in Japan.

THE LIFE OF THE BUSINESSMAN

For the Japanese businessman, a demon for work to the extent of being called a workaholic, work comes first, and many feel guilty if time away is taken for personal reasons. Usual work hours are 9: 00–5:00, but even when departing long past then, custom demands an apology for leaving first if others are still working.

In cities like Tokyo and Osaka, where land is prohibitively high, the common practice is to live in the suburbs, so that a two-hour commute (one way) is not unusual and, like the return trip late at night, is made on a jam-packed train, often while standing up.

An important part of the businessman's work is spending time with co-workers after working hours. Usually this means dropping in a bar where, over drinks, work-related matters, relationships and complaints can be talked over. Many dispel the day's cares by loudly singing, a diversion so widespread that there are bars equipped to cater to it. Back home often in the wee hours, it's off to bed exhausted and on an empty stomach. Days off force a choice between recuperating or doing right by the family by taking them out for a day together.

◀(left) **Commuter Train** Rush hours find these trains so over-crowded that boarding is impossible at times. Nevertheless, many riders use the time to catch up on their reading.

▼(lower left)**Station Bike Lot** As homes get farther from commuter stations, more people go there on bikes and mopeds. Congestion and complaints abound.

▼(lower right) **Stand-up Diner** After leaving the house early on an empty stomach, some workers substitute a quick bowl of noodles for breakfast.

▲**Morning at Tokyo Station**   Jam-packed commuter trains disgorge office workers heading for work in Tokyo's business district.

▲**Red-lantern Bar**   When working hours are over, office workers often head for these low-priced watering holes to drink and dispel the day's cares.

▲**A Businessman's Day Off**   The daily routine of leaving home early and returning late offers precious little time for family togetherness except on a day off.

● THE BUSINESSMAN AND
THE TDU SYSTEM
(TEMPORARY DISPATCH, UNACCOMPANIED)

The Japanese businessman is subject to transfer, and compliance is the usual response whether it takes him from the main office to a branch, vice-versa, or to a post abroad.

For young singles a transfer may be no problem, but for the married man with a home and children in school, it can mean making the transfer alone.

Of the two main reasons for this, the first concerns the children's education, for if they are in junior or senior high school, crucial examinations lie just ahead. To leave them behind with the wife is thus to their advantage. The second problem is the home. Having finally obtained one, the wife is loath to give it up. Importance is thus put on educational advancement and the house, even at the expense of family separation.

At present there are as many as 150,000 such families each year, so that the TDU system is fast becoming a social problem which, some say, can be traced to industry's doorstep.

▲TDU System employees return tired from work to the lonely tasks of cooking and housework.

93

WORKING WOMEN

Economic growth and changes in the make-up of industry have brought an increasing number of women out of the traditional workplaces of home and field. Noticeable too are the higher numbers of middle-aged and older workers, higher educational backgrounds and lengthening years of work.

Instead of working up to the time of marriage or childbirth, more women are now electing to be working wives and mothers. Others are choosing careers over marriage. A recent survey showed that working women now outnumber those in the home.

By industry, over 80% of working women are in the service, manufacturing and sales sectors, mostly as clerical and production workers. Housewives with part-time jobs are also on the increase. In fact, women now account for 35% of the labor force, though in general earn less than men and have fewer opportunities for advancement.

▲**Teacher**   Teaching has long been a popular occupation for women, with many in the primary schools and increasing numbers serving as principals.

▲**Clerical worker**   The biggest occupation for women is in clerical work. As office automation progresses, more and more women are doing work involving word processors, computers and other machines of the information age.

▶**Policewoman**   Women serve as kind and friendly officers of the law, giving children lessons in safety and handling parking violations.

▲**Women Managers** Women as company presidents and executives are increasing, even being promoted to upper echelon positions in government service.

▲**Programmer** Women in technical jobs such as programmers and systems engineers are increasing as computers become more widespread.

▲**Supermarket Check-out Clerk** A great many working women are part-timers in a wide range of jobs such as checkers, cashiers, clerks.

▲**Farm Housewife** Increased mechanization and lessened manual labor find more wives running the farms while husbands work full or part-time elsewhere.

▲**Women Workers at a Canning Factory** Many women are employed at simple jobs in production processes.

▲**Tea Ceremony Teacher** Women accomplished in the tea ceremony or flower arrangement earn money and find pleasure in teaching at home or at culture centers.

CHILDREN AND THE WAR FOR EDUCATION

Japanese children of today differ from those of earlier generations in that they live in an age of abundance: plenty of toys, books, and, despite the smallness of Japanese houses, plenty of space in which to study. No space may be had for Dad's den or Mom's workroom, but invariably the child has his or her inner sanctum.

Most students (97%) go on to high school after the first nine years of mandatory education, and of them 46% go on to higher learning. To get the child into one of Japan's 500 universities (preferably of a higher level), the entire family unites to create an environment conducive to study, for acceptance by a good university eases the way to employment with a prestigious company, which is the ultimate goal. The campaign can even begin before kindergarten, with the child studying Japanese and Math at a special school or taking private lessons on the piano, abacus or in swimming. Once into the higher grades of primary school, students attending "after-school schools" (*juku*) increase to as high as 60% in urban areas. Some even sacrifice weekends to attend.

Aspirants to prestigious high schools and universities follow suit by attending cram schools and prep schools after regular school hours and/or receiving private tutoring, all in the hopes of winning the war against the entrance examinations.

▲ **Piano Lessons**　Some 70% of primary school students take private lessons in one thing or another (swimming, piano, abacus, etc.), and many study more than one.

Advancement

(%)　　High school ——　　University ——

| | 90.8 | 92.6 | 93.5 | 94.2 | 94.3 | |
| 89.4 | 91.9 | 93.1 | 94.0 | 94.3 | 94.3 | 94.4 |

| 32.2 | 37.8 | 37.7 | 37.4 | 36.9 | 35.1 |
| 34.7 | 38.6 | 38.4 | 37.4 | 36.3 |

1973 74　75　76　77　78　79　80　81　82　83

▲ ***Juku* Pick-up and Delivery**　After regular school is over, students quickly head for *juku* to study until as late as 9:00 p.m. To encourage them, parents often take or pick them up in the family car.

▲**Toy Department**   There is a never-ending stream of expensive games for sale, and hordes of children descend on such departments on days off in their never-ending search for the newest and the latest.

▲**A Child's Room**   Many children get their own room once they begin primary school. With an abundance of books and toys, perhaps a piano and/or a stereo, etc., the child would seem to outrank the head of the house.

▲**Entrance Examination**   Difficult examinations await aspirants to well-known schools. The support of the entire family is needed and provided.

▲**Juku**   Studying at these privately-run schools may begin from childhood. With too much to study at regular schools, such outside study is about the only way to pass the entrance examinations.

▼**Home Tutor**   Students from prestigious universities are often employed to give one-on-one tutoring at home.

THE JAPANESE AT LEISURE

The old work ethic of Japan made working from dawn to dusk a virtue. The concept of enjoying leisure was, in fact, almost nil. Even in the high economic growth era prior to the oil crisis, time off was largely ignored and overtime was a given, making it safe to say that in the popular consciousness no room existed for the enjoyment of leisure and that the Japanese are not particularly adept at it. Such passive actions as watching TV or resting account for most of it. Of late, however, with reduced workhours, the spread of a two-day weekend, and days off in summer and winter, the idea is taking root that leisure is a thing to be actively enjoyed. Yet a proclivity for fads and conformity has the Japanese flocking to the same well-known recreation areas in such hordes that traffic jams, long lines and sheer crushes of humanity exhaust rather than refresh them.

Japanese-style leisure also seems to be a kind of "service" to one's family by the husband. What is needed are more and better facilities and an individualized approach to the enjoyment of leisure.

▲**Heavy Traffic** In the "on" season when people head for vacation areas, roads are so crowded that motorists are exhausted before reaching their destinations.

▲**Amusement Park** Families with youngsters fill such playlands on weekends, holidays and days off. Some parks have an annual attendance of 10 million.

▲**Swimming at the Beach**   In summer the beaches are people, people, people, with hardly any elbow room. Everyone wants to go where everyone else wants to go.

◀**Golf-driving Range**   People like to practice before going out on the green, and many middle-aged men find the practice is also a good way to keep fit on days off.

▲*Pachinko*   A uniquely Japanese game played with a small amount of money. Parlors are crowded during lunch hours and on non-working days.

▼**Tennis**   Like golf, tennis is also highly popular.

▲**Pedestrian Mall**   Busy downtown areas are closed to vehicles on Sundays and holidays so that pedestrians can enjoy shopping and strolling.

URBAN AND RURAL AREAS

As the economy rapidly developed and industrialization advanced, the cities required large work forces so that by the latter half of the 1950s the population came to center in them. In rural areas, where jobs and cash wages were scarce, people unable to endure life there while elsewhere modernization was bringing improvements in the standard of living migrated to the cities in droves.

Drained of their youth, many rural areas took on the status of depopulated zones and found themselves in dire straits when it came to production, natural disasters, education and medical care. Hard hit were the off-shore islands, the deep-snow country, towns and villages.

The urban population increase has given rise to cramped housing, traffic congestion, insufficient educational facilities, inadequate sewerage systems and a host of pollution problems. To help resolve them, programs are underway to disperse factories and universities from metropolitan areas, radically re-think city planning, and put up more high-rise buildings as part of urban renewal.

Population Of The Three Major Metropolitan Areas

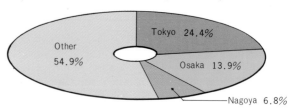

Other 54.9%
Tokyo 24.4%
Osaka 13.9%
Nagoya 6.8%

▲ **Rush-hour Traffic** Snarled, congested traffic is a given in downtown areas.

▲**Tokyo at Night** Eating and drinking establishments are near the business districts, and workers on the way home make the most of them until the wee hours.

▲**Daytime in Tokyo** Offices, department stores and universities abound. So do businessmen, shoppers and students. (Shibuya)

▲**Tsukuba Academic New Town** National experimental and research institutions have been relocated to this huge academic town built in a prefecture bordering Tokyo to relieve the capital of its burgeoning population.

▶(left) **Urban Renewal (Sumida, Tokyo)** Clusters of high-rises stand where old wooden houses once were jammed.

▶(right) **Reviving the Countryside (Shimane Pref.)** Steps include making industry areas to attract firms and promote local production.

▲**Home Construction** Fields on city outskirts are giving way to housing developments and bringing into focus the problem of the destruction of nature.

▲**Depopulated Village** Many people have forsaken their homes deep in the mountain villages to go to the cities.

THE OLD AND THE NEW

Respect for tradition has long been practiced in Japan, where culture, crafts and customs hark back into remote history. An island nation never once invaded, Japan retained its unique culture.

There was a shift, however, under the cultural influx following World War II. Durable goods (TVs, washing machines, cars, telephones, etc.) rapidly spread as economic conditions eased. Houses, once large, dark and shared by the extended family, gave way to smaller, brighter, western-style ones. Food became instant, frozen, ready-made, so that eating habits too were streamlined.

Yet Japan retains much that is traditional. The computer in the home sits next to the Buddhist altar; the decorative alcove holds the stereo or TV; one step inside the western-style front porch is a room floored with *tatami*. Weddings start with the bride in kimono but midway have her in a wedding dress and at the end in a travel suit. Auspicious days for weddings, funerals and other events are chosen after consulting the old calendar. Ground-breaking for a high-tech factory begins with a ritual by a Shinto priest. Overall, modern-day Japan is a rich mix of the old and the new.

▲**Shrine within a Building**   On streets lined with modern buildings, on skyscraper rooftops and elsewhere, shrines are built to seek divine help in business success.

▲**Blessing of the Land**   Before construction work on new buildings commences, prayers are offered for divine protection. High-tech factories are no exception.

▲**Wedding Ceremony**   The luxurious old-style kimono, the ritual exchange of wine before the altar and other vestiges of the old wedding rites still remain.

▲*Kado* **(gate)** *matsu* **(pine)**   During New Year's these traditional pine decorations to welcome the year's deity are seen even at modern buildings and companies.

▲*Shichi* **(7)** *Go* **(5)** *San* **(3)**   To celebrate their third, fifth and seventh years of age, children dress in kimono and go to shrines to offer thanks.

▲**Living Room**   In not a few homes the living room floor is *tatami* mats, and in what used to be the decorative alcove now stand the family TV, stereo, PC and VCR.

▲**Buddhist Altar**   It is still the custom to install a Buddhist altar within the home dedicated to the memory of the departed and to offer flowers, food and prayers.

FESTIVALS

The Japanese, a people with an agricultural heritage, hold many festivals, mainly in spring for planting and in fall for harvesting. At the start of a year or a season, people pray for a time of plenty or for protection from natural disasters.

Seasonal festivals include those rooted in religious tradition, those to mark community, economic or political events, and those of commerce and industry. Indeed, the word "festival" is nowadays affixed to so many non-events (i. e., hotspring "festival", sightseeing "festival") that it has all but lost its true meaning.

Most true festivals are held at shrines and are distinguished by a veneration of ancestors, for it is a tenet of faith in Japan that our life and well-being flow from that source.

The original significance of festivals has now faded and some have even disappeared. There is, though, an increase in large-scale "festivals" of a commercial nature.

▲ **Sagicho** Straw streamers and pine boughs that decorate homes over the New Year period are burned to speed the year's deity on its way. (Shiga Prefecture)

◄ **Shiogama Port Festival** A gaily decorated ship with a portable shrine on board goes around the bay as part of a sea festival. (Shiogama, Miyagi Prefecture)

▼ **kanda Festival** A festival in the middle of May in which local deities are transported around their parishes in portable shrines. (Asakusa, Tokyo)

▲ *Gion* Festival   Contagious diseases prevalent in summer are blamed on the god of sickness. To control the deity, a festival is held in July for about a month. (Kyoto)

▲ *Nebuta*   This procession, famous for its decorations emblazoned with likenesses of kabuki actors, is a supplication for good health. (Aomori Pref.)

▲*Yatsushikaodori*   When the autumn harvest is in, even the deer come down from the mountains to celebrate. The dance   expresses that joy. (Uwajima, Ehime Pref.)

TRADITIONAL INDUSTRIES(1)

Many localities in Japan have industries that arose from techniques passed down over the ages. The name of the producing area is often incorporated into the name of the product itself, hence *Wajima* lacquerware, *Nishijin* cloth, *Tosa* paper, *Kutani* pottery. The use of local raw materials imparts a characteristic touch to each product, whose production in feudal times was promoted and protected by the local lord as a means of enriching the fief's coffers, with trade secrets kept tightly within the realm.

Unlike modern-day methods, production in traditional industries involves little reliance on machinery, employs simple tools, and turns out items one at a time. The result is various goods in small quantities, each with a distinctive stamp. One factory may employ 2–3 people or, at most, 30, and be a one-family affair where work is performed in one section of the home. Items thus made convey an individuality and charm unattainable in mass-produced goods.

①Lacquered box
(Tsugaru, Aomori)

②Iron kettle
(Nambu-Iwate)

⑦Woven cloth
(Yuki, Ibaraki)

⑧Pottery pot
(Mashiko, Tochigi)

⑬Wood carving
(Kamakura, Kanagawa)

⑭Woven cloth
(Ojiya, Niigata)

⑱Tie-dyed cloth
(Narumi, Aichi)

⑲Wood carving
(Gifu)

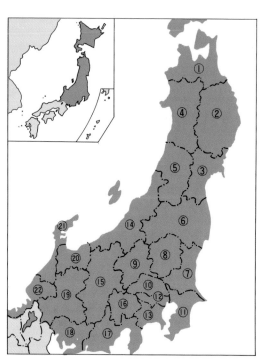

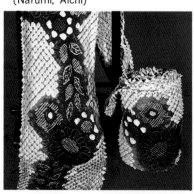

● Traditional Crafts of Eastern Japan

③*Kokeshi* doll
　(Miyagi)

④Bark overlay
　(Akita)

⑤Handwoven cloth
　(Yamagata)

⑥Lacquerware
　(Aidzu, Fukushima)

⑨Woven cloth
　(Kiryu, Gunma)

⑩Doll
　(Iwatsuki, Saitama)

⑪Fans
　(Boshu-Chiba)

⑫Dyed cloth
　(Tokyo)

⑮Buddhist altar
　(Iiyama, Nagano)

⑯Rock-crystal figure
　(Koshu-Yamanashi)

⑰Bamboo basket
　(Suruga-Shizuoka)

⑳*Inami* carving
　(Inami, Toyama)

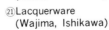
㉑Lacquerware
　(Wajima, Ishikawa)

㉒Japanese paper
　(Echizen-Fukui)

TRADITIONAL INDUSTRIES (2)

Traditional crafts and their production are mostly governed by the raw materials locally available and the suitability of the area's climate. Both lacquerware and weaving, for example, developed in areas of high humidity due to their special needs. Even so, the locale retaining the largest number and variety of Japan's traditional crafts is Kyoto.

In recent years, some crafts have seen an increasing reliance on imported raw materials. Others, due to a reputation for highly skilled craftsmanship and originality, have almost priced themselves out of a market. With mastery of some crafts taking 10 years or more, few people are willing to take them up, and the present craftsmen themselves are no longer young. Modernizing and mechanizing without losing the traditional touch is another thorny problem.

To help resolve these problems, legislation has been enacted to promote and protect the industry, and localities are taking steps to consolidate factories, streamline production and shipping, and establish research and training centers.

㉓Plaited cords
(Iga, Mie)

㉔Potteryware
(Shigaraki, Shiga)

㉙Lacquerware
(Kishu- Wakayama)

㉚Colored paper
(Inshu-Tottori)

㉟Dyed cotton cloth
(Awa-Tokushima)

㊱Lacquerware
(Kagawa)

㊶Potteryware
(Hasami, Nagasaki)

㊷Lantern
(Yamaga, Kumamoto)

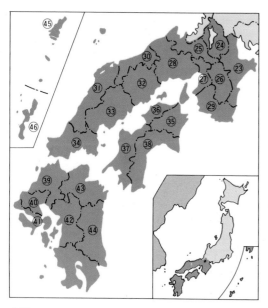

●Traditional Crafts of Western Japan

㉕ *Nishijin* cloth
(Kyoto)

㉖Tea whisk
(Takayama, Nara)

㉗Cutlery
(Sakai, Osaka)

㉘Abacus
(Banshu-Hyogo)

㉛Stone lantern
(Idzumo-Shimane)

㉜Pottery
(Bizen-Okayama)

㉝Writing brushes
(Kumano, Hiroshima)

㉞Inkstone
(Akama, Yamaguchi)

㊲China plate
(Tobe, Ehime)

㊳Japanese paper
(Tosa-Kochi)

㊴Doll
(Hakata, Fukuoka)

㊵China vase
(Imari/Arita, Saga)

㊸Bamboo vaseholder
(Beppu, Oita)

㊹Go stones
(Hyuga-Miyazaki)

㊺Woven cloth
(Oshima, Kagoshima)

㊻Woven cloth
(Yomitanzan, Okinawa)

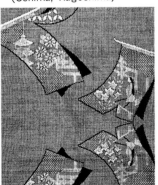

POPULATION AND THE AGING OF SOCIETY

Japan's population was 35 million at the turn of the century, 100 million in 1967, and is 120 million at present. Through higher standards in living, medical care and public health, Japan now has the highest life expectancy in the world: 74.5 years for men, 80.1 for women.

The UN has classified nations as being "young" if less than 4% of the total population are 65 or over, as "mature" when 4-7% are over 65, and as "aged" when 7% exceed that figure. Japan entered the latter category in 1970 due to its declining death and birth rates, which have accelerated the aging of the population. The elderly have increased since then, and will exceed the 20% mark by 2015, a rate faster than in other countries.

The ratio of the productive population (15-64) to the young (0-14) and the old (over 65) is increasing as society ages. Today, 10 working people have a dependency burden of 3.5 children and 1.3 aged people, but in 2000 it will be 3 children and 3.5 aged people. Future problems are whether workers can support such a load and whether medical care and pension plans for the aged can be maintained.

▲**Oldsters Enjoying Tennis**   Tennis clubs have seen a recent rise in older members who like to keep active as a way of maintaining their health, even taking on young players.

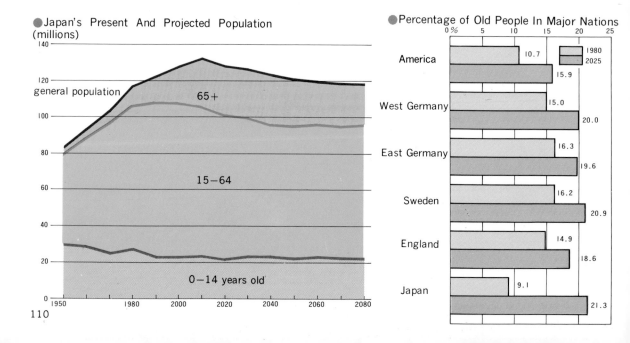

●Japan's Present And Projected Population (millions)

general population

65+

15—64

0—14 years old

●Percentage of Old People In Major Nations

	1980	2025
America	10.7	15.9
West Germany	15.0	20.0
East Germany	16.3	19.6
Sweden	16.2	20.9
England	14.9	18.6
Japan	9.1	21.3

● WANTED: A LIFE WORTH LIVING

In 1947 life expectancy was 50 years for a man, 47 for a woman. Today it is 80 years, so that the period after childrearing has lengthened. How best to spend those years is a major concern for both the aged and society at large.

To provide employment opportunities for those senior citizens desiring work, special employment agencies have been established around the nation. In a society geared for activity, it is important to utilize the talents of the elderly and to provide opportunities for earning an income so as to encourage them to enjoy a healthy and worthwhile life.

For those who seek to find value in life through continued education, many municipalities have opened so-called "Silver Schools."

▲**Job for the Elderly**   Pond-cleaning is part of park maintenance work obtained via agencies for the aged.

▲**Gateball**   Elderly residents of a neighborhood get together to enjoy light sports such as gateball. Japan has many such clubs.

▲**Silver School Chorus**   Group get-togethers sponsored by local municipalities are enthusiastically attended and give pleasure in life.

▲ **The Young and the Old**   Despite the rise in nuclear families, many elderly parents live with their children, taking care of the house and grandchildren while the younger people hold down jobs. Keeping busy in this way is a source of their good health.

▲**Old People's Home**   Condominiums specially equipped with medical care facilities for the elderly have gained popularity as places to spend the later years of life.

A SAFE JAPAN

Japan, with its stability, peace and order and low incidence of crime, is often cited as the world's safest nation.

Ubiquitous but minuscule sub-stations, commonly called police boxes, with an officer always on duty, are a singularly Japanese system and underlie the entire police network. The on-duty officer's functions range from patrolling his area to handling crimes that occur within it, plus regulating traffic. Addressed familiarly by the residents, he cultivates a rapport with them and acts as an important point of contact with the police.

Japan, however, is in no way safe in regard to such natural disasters as earthquakes, forest fires and typhoons, even though scientific advances in early-warning systems and coping methods have done much to minimize their damage.

In a society grown complex, safety too is complex, so that not only the police or fire departments but businesses and individuals too must take steps. The growth in security firms offering computer-aided 24–hour surveillance reflects this.

Emergency Disaster Information Center Data collected from local areas is analyzed in preparation for sudden disasters. Private-sector safety firms are flourishing.

Koban (police box) There's one in every busy area. Residents are familiar with them as sources of crime prevention, information and safety instruction.

Neighborhood Patrol Police make their rounds checking for locked doors and providing lessons in safety as part of crime prevention work.

JAPAN IN CHARTS AND GRAPHS

FARMING/FORESTRY/WATER

●Food Production Self-sufficiency

The food self-sufficiency rate has fallen, especially in cereals where those for food went from 80 in 1965 to 69 in 1982, and those for feed from 61 to 33, with the result that the rate in farm products has gone from 83 to 73.   One reason is the dietary increase in bread and meat, for which wheat and feed are mostly imported.   Another is the agricultural structure: almost no wheat and soy beans are grown.

● Self-sufficiency Rates of Major Nations

The rates are high in the advanced nations of Europe and America where, for trade or food stability reasons, emphasis is put on food production, which is promoted through safeguards and supports.

● Farm Households

The number has dropped from 6 million to 4.5 million, mainly in full-time farming, while even many part-time farmers derive their primary income from a source other than farming. Most farmers have an average of a little less than 1 ha under cultivation, although farms of more than 2-3 ha have increased.

■Self-sufficiency in Farm Food Products

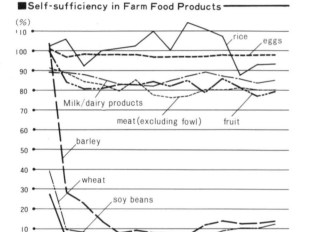

■Major Nations Self-sufficiency in Farm Food Products

item　　　nation		Japan	USA	England	W. Germany	France	Denmark	Canada
Cereals		33	162	77	90	170	113	183
Potatoes		96	110	96	88	104	132	83
Beans		7	142	81	17	69	82	79
Vegetables		97	99	79	33	93	70	68
Meat		81	97	71	86	92	298	100
Milk/ dairy products		86	93	83	106	110	194	97
Oil		29	181	17	40	51	77	91

＝1978＝ (%)

■Farm Households : Full/Part-time

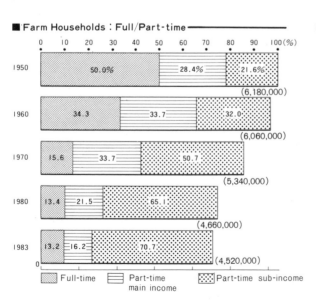

■Farm Households & Cultivated Acreage

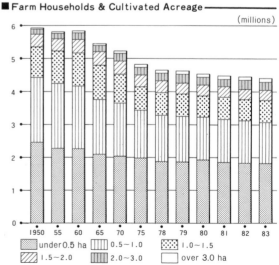

● **Farm Mechanization** Most planting, weeding and harvesting is mechanized except where equipment is difficult to use. The spread of machines, as, for example, transplanting machines, made wheat cultivation difficult and was a primary factor in its abandonment. Also, purchases of expensive but potentially useless machines put a heavy strain on farmers' finances.

On the plus side, mechanization has lightened farm work and no doubt will expand as farms enlarge and part-time farmers increase.

● **Fertilizer-intensive Farming/Land Use** Japan uses comparatively more fertilizer than other nations do. Farmers once used such organic materials as human waste, manure, garbage and weeds, supplementing them with chemical fertilizers; but due to industrial advances synthetic fertilizers are cheaply available. Also, manure is hard to come by, as livestock is fast disappearing from farms, places to raise animals are being taken by encroaching cities, and part-time farmers simply have no time. The handier chemical fertilizers have thus become the main ones, with the result that the soil has deteriorated. This in turn has led to reconsiderations on the use of organic fertilizers.

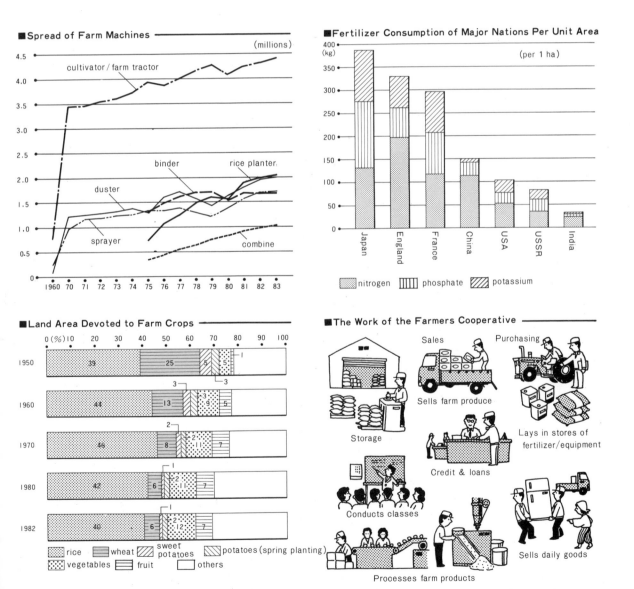

■ Spread of Farm Machines

(millions)

cultivator / farm tractor

binder   rice planter

duster

sprayer

combine

1960 70 71 72 73 74 75 76 77 78 79 80 81 82 83

■ Fertilizer Consumption of Major Nations Per Unit Area

400
(kg)   (per 1 ha)
350
300
250
200
150
100
50
0

Japan England France China USA USSR India

▨ nitrogen   ∭ phosphate   ▨ potassium

■ Land Area Devoted to Farm Crops

0 (%)10 20 30 40 50 60 70 80 90 100

1950   39   25   5   5   1

1960   44   13   3   9   5   3 3

1970   46   8   2 11   7   2

1980   42   6   2   7   1

1982   40   6   2   7   1

▨ rice   ▨ wheat   ▨ sweet potatoes   ▨ potatoes (spring planting)
▨ vegetables   ▤ fruit   ☐ others

■ The Work of the Farmers Cooperative

Sales   Purchasing

Sells farm produce

Storage   Lays in stores of
                         fertilizer/equipment

                Credit & loans

Conducts classes

                                    Sells daily goods

Processes farm products

● **Rice**   Rice is an important food for the Japanese and the most important crop in farming. The various stages of its growth in the paddies also form part of the Japanese aesthetic.

With rice long at the core of farming, techniques have improved so that the average yield per 10 a is 500kg. Until now, most farming was done on less than 1 ha of land, but due to mechanization and the ease with which it can be done, farming on less than 0.5 ha accounts for 60% of it.

● **Potatoes/Sweet Potatoes**   In Japan, the potato is not the all-important tuber that it is in the West. Most are grown in Hokkaido for food or processing, with only a small portion used as fodder. Sweet potatoes are mainly produced in Kagoshima. Consumption is low but stable. Japan is self-sufficient in both types.

● **Vegetables**   Japan is a veritable vegetable garden. Due to the proliferation of hot-house culture, a variety of vegetables can be enjoyed year round. Most vegetable farming is done on a small scale, with 80% done on land of less than 10 a.

● **Fruit**   Japan produces a variety of fruit year round. That, plus the proliferation of hot-house culturing and imports make the nation a veritable fruit basket.

■ Land In Rice/Harvest/Yield Per 10 a

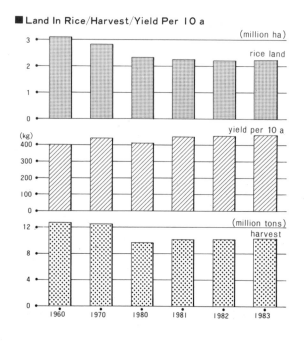

■ Production of Potatoes/Sweet Potatoes

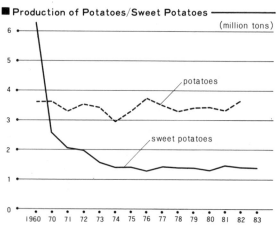

■ Rice Imports/Exports

■ Vegetable Production

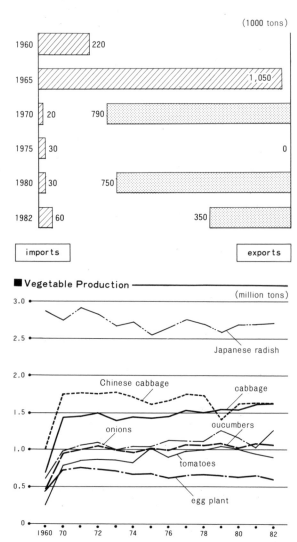

Especially plentiful are tangerines and apples. By a government policy of getting farmers to utilize rice paddies, tangerine production was promoted but resulted in such a surfeit that a shift to other products is being encouraged. Grapefruit and oranges are imported, but are putting citrus growers in a difficult position.

A wide range of apples is grown to suit consumers' tastes. The current one now is a large, sweet-tasting apple. Pears (both Japanese and Western ones) are readily available, as are various types of grapes.

● **Livestock**　　Along with rice production, livestock ranks as a hefty income-

earner for farmers and has seen big changes.

Large-scale breeding farms have replaced the familiar backyards holding a few pigs and chickens. This has also led to a reluctant reliance on imported feed, which underscores agriculture's weakening position.

However, such large-scale ventures assure a large and stable supply of meat, eggs and other foodstuffs, mostly inexpensively, so that the Japanese intake of animal protein has soared.

■ **Fruit Production**

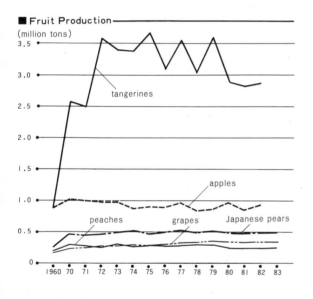

■ **Fruit Imports**　　=1982=

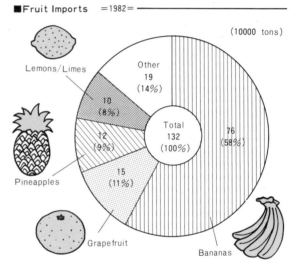

■ **Livestock**

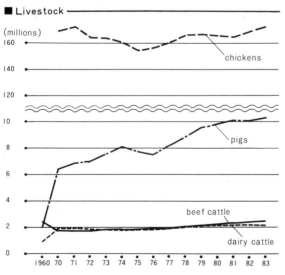

■ **Livestock Feed**

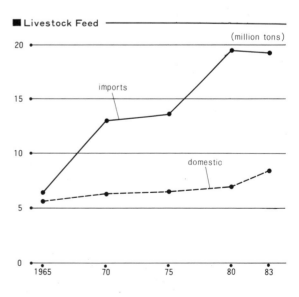

● **Forests**　　Forests cover two-thirds of the nation. Their restful, restorative powers have long been appreciated, as have their role in fostering water resources, though in recent years this awareness would seem to be fading. The forestry industry, on the other hand, is gradually losing its workers since it cannot provide sufficient work to sustain a livelihood over an extended period of time. It is important, however, in both the material and psychological sense, to continue to preserve and maintain our precious forests. Long-term planning and management are therefore essential.

● **Lumber**　　Because proper forest management was not followed, lumber production today is on the decline. Also, reforestation after felling was mainly done with fast-growing, easy-to-handle coniferous trees, so that the broad-leaved trees, which are more suited to Japan's climate, are decreasing. The demand for wood in present-day Japan is enormous. Diverse and numerous uses include those for construction, pulp and plywood. Accordingly, imports exceed domestic production and Japan has become one of the few wood-

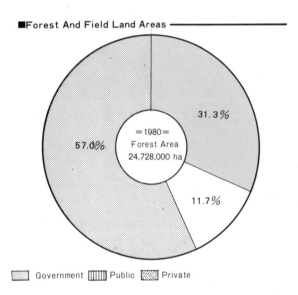

■Forest And Field Land Areas

=1980=
Forest Area
24,728,000 ha

57.0%　　31.3%　　11.7%

☐ Government　▥ Public　▨ Private

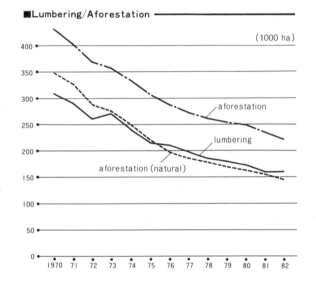

■Lumbering/Aforestation

(1000 ha)

aforestation
lumbering
aforestation (natural)

1970　71　72　73　74　75　76　77　78　79　80　81　82

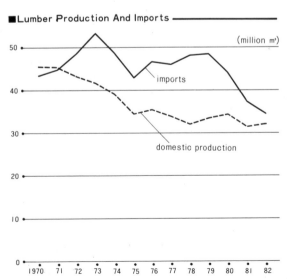

■Lumber Production And Imports

(million m³)

imports

domestic production

1970　71　72　73　74　75　76　77　78　79　80　81　82

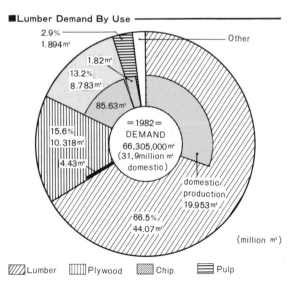

■Lumber Demand By Use

2.9%
1.894 m³

1.82 m³
13.2%
8.783 m³

85.63 m³

15.6%
10.318 m³

4.43 m³

=1982=
DEMAND
66,305,000 m³
(31.9million m³ domestic)

Other

domestic production
19.953 m³

66.5%
44.07 m³

(million m³)

▨ Lumber　▥ Plywood　▨ Chip　☰ Pulp

118

importing nations in the world. Imports from southeast Asia have increased so much that felling trees there has led to flooding and climatic changes.

● **Fisheries** Japan is surrounded by seas, is rich in marine resources, and can claim catches that consistently keep her in a top position worldwide, with both Japan and the USSR vastly outdistancing the closest contenders.

The industry itself has been re-organized and expanded through bigger ships, modern equipment, and improved gear and methods, gradually shifting from coastal to off-shore to deep-sea fishing. This in turn has led to indiscriminate fishing and heightened friction with various nations, so that negotiations on catches have had to be undertaken. Japan's fishing industry has also been increasingly restricted by the adoption by many nations of the 200-mile economic fishing zone, and further by the jump in oil prices.

One result is renewed attention to coastal and off-shore fishing and the adoption of aquaculture.

■ Catches Of Major Nations

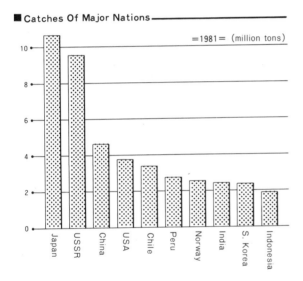

■ Catch By Type Of Fishery

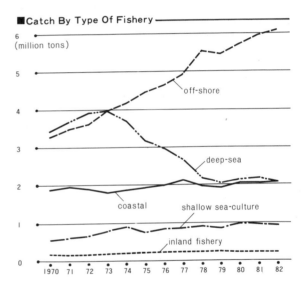

■ Catch By Type

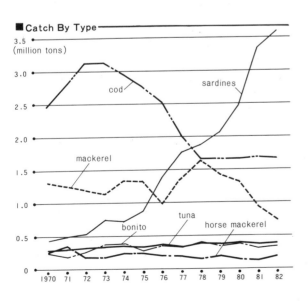

■ Fish Usage (including imports) =1982= (million tons)   ( )=%

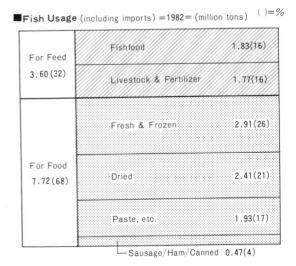

For Feed 3.60 (32)	Fishfood	1.83(16)
	Livestock & Fertilizer	1.77(16)
For Food 7.72 (68)	Fresh & Frozen	2.91(26)
	Dried	2.41(21)
	Paste, etc.	1.93(17)

└─Sausage/Ham/Canned 0.47(4)

MINING & ENERGY

● **Minerals** Japan produces a variety of minerals, though output is small (except in limestone and other raw materials for cement) so that the many minerals industry needs as raw materials and fuels are imported.

The imports come mainly from the developing nations, where Japan provides advanced technological know-how and co-operates with the nations for local economic development to ensure a stable supply of needed minerals.

● **Energy Consumption** The higher a nation's standard of living, the more energy it consumes per capita. The high consumption in America and Canada is due not only to vigorous production activity and the high standard of living but also to the hugeness of the land area and the great amount of energy produced domestically.

Japan, however, with the world's second largest GNP (excluding the USSR), consumes less energy. With a population large in relation to the limited land area, a high level of economic activity can be enjoyed without as much energy consumption.

● **Energy Dependency** A look at how Japan obtains its energy supplies reveals an

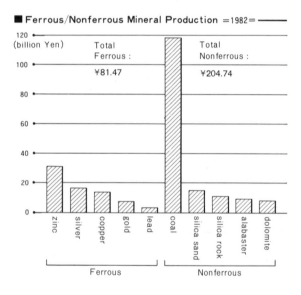

■ Ferrous/Nonferrous Mineral Production =1982=

Total Ferrous : ¥81.47

Total Nonferrous : ¥204.74

Ferrous: zinc, silver, copper, gold, lead, coal

Nonferrous: silica sand, silica rock, alabaster, dolomite

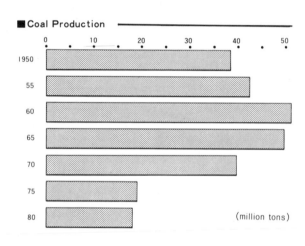

■ Coal Production

(million tons)

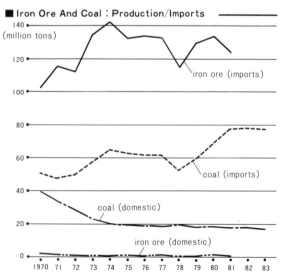

■ Iron Ore And Coal : Production/Imports

iron ore (imports)

coal (imports)

coal (domestic)

iron ore (domestic)

1970 71 72 73 74 75 76 77 78 79 80 81 82 83

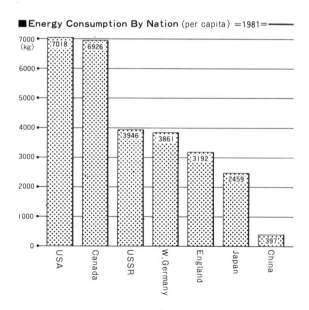

■ Energy Consumption By Nation (per capita) =1981=

USA	Canada	USSR	W. Germany	England	Japan	China
7018	6926	3946	3861	3192	2459	397

extreme dependency on foreign sources in comparison with other nations. Hydropower is practically the only purely domestic source, while most oil and natural gas are imported, as is much of the coal. Electricity, though generated domestically, relies on fuel imports for both thermal and nuclear power stations.

Such dependency on foreign nations for everyday energy needs reveals a decided vulnerability. Accordingly, strong efforts have been made for energy savings, alternate energy development, oil reserves and storage and other measures. In the indus-

trial sector, energy savings are already showing results, but R&D in alternate sources is difficult in the extreme because oil is still the cheapest. Stockpiling was pursued in earnest but for a short period, as prices since the oil crisis have dropped due to a worldwide glut. How long it will continue is anyone's guess. There is also no guarantee that conflict will not erupt in the Middle East. Accordingly, it behooves Japan to continue its domestic policies of counter-measures.

■ Energy Supplies

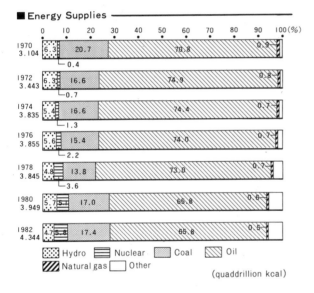

■ Imports Of Oil/Oil Products

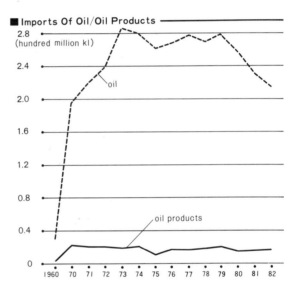

■ Electric Power Generation

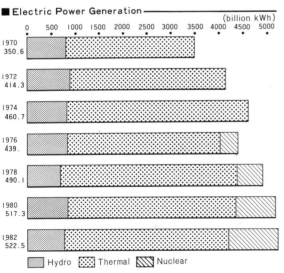

■ City Gas Production

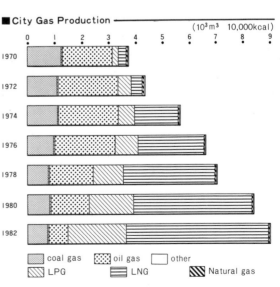

MANUFACTURING AND CONSTRUCTION

● World's No. 2 Industrial Nation

The manufacturing industry grew rapidly from its heavy-chemicals base and, excluding the USSR, is second only to America. Although the two oil crises of the '70s dulled both economic growth and industrial output, Japan has kept its No. 2 position.

● Large and Small Enterprises

Small-and-medium-size companies occupy a major share of industry. Firms with under 300 workers account for 99%, employees for 73%, and shipments for 52%, with little change in the last 10 or even 20 years.

Most small-and-medium-size firms are subcontractors of big enterprises. The two sectors, in fact, are mutually dependent, sometimes co-operating, sometimes competing, with the larger at times safeguarding and promoting the smaller, who in turn often venture into areas not engaged in by the larger to successfully develop new and advanced products. The robustness of these small firms is actually a major factor in Japan's standing as the world's second-largest industrial power.

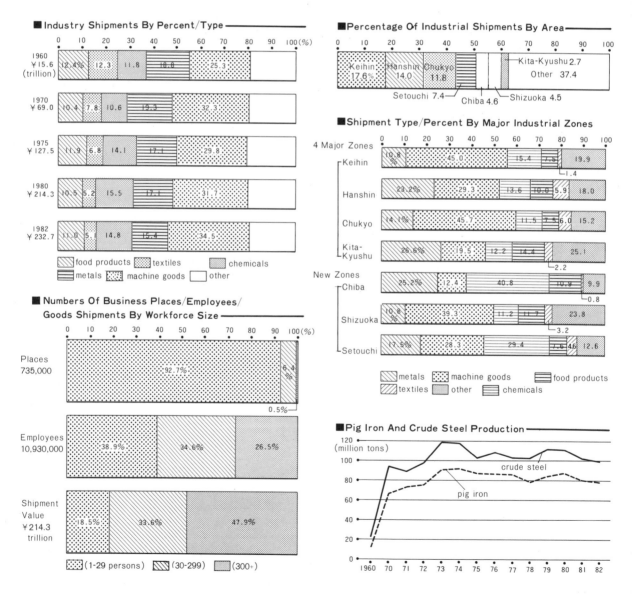

■ Industry Shipments By Percent/Type

| | food products | textiles | chemicals |
| metals | machine goods | other |

1960 ¥15.6 (trillion): 12.4% / 12.3 / 11.8 / 18.0 / 25.3

1970 ¥69.0: 10.4 / 7.8 / 10.6 / 19.3 / 32.3

1975 ¥127.5: 11.9 / 6.8 / 14.1 / 17.1 / 29.8

1980 ¥214.3: 10.5 / 5.2 / 15.5 / 17.1 / 31.7

1982 ¥232.7: 11.0 / 5.1 / 14.8 / 15.4 / 34.5

■ Numbers Of Business Places/Employees/ Goods Shipments By Workforce Size

Places 735,000: 92.7% / 6.4% / 0.5%

Employees 10,930,000: 38.9% / 34.6% / 26.5%

Shipment Value ¥214.3 trillion: 18.5% / 33.6% / 47.9%

(1-29 persons) (30-299) (300+)

■ Percentage Of Industrial Shipments By Area

Keihin 17.6% / Hanshin 14.0 / Chukyo 11.8 / Setouchi 7.4 / Chiba 4.6 / Shizuoka 4.5 / Kita-Kyushu 2.7 / Other 37.4

■ Shipment Type/Percent By Major Industrial Zones

4 Major Zones
- Keihin: 10.8% / 45.0 / 15.4 / 7.5 / 1.4 / 19.9
- Hanshin: 23.2% / 29.3 / 13.6 / 10.0 / 5.9 / 18.0
- Chukyo: 14.1% / 45.7 / 11.5 / 7.5 / 6.0 / 15.2
- Kita-Kyushu: 26.6% / 19.5 / 12.2 / 14.4 / 2.2 / 25.1

New Zones
- Chiba: 25.2% / 12.4 / 40.8 / 10.9 / 0.8 / 9.9
- Shizuoka: 10.8% / 39.3 / 11.2 / 11.7 / 3.2 / 23.8
- Setouchi: 17.5% / 28.3 / 29.4 / 7.6 / 4.6 / 12.6

 metals   machine goods   food products
 textiles   other   chemicals

■ Pig Iron And Crude Steel Production

crude steel

pig iron

1960 70 71 72 73 74 75 76 77 78 79 80 81 82

● **Automobile Industry Growth**   Car production in the '70s, despite cost rises induced by the oil crisis, heightened its competitive edge by technological advances and improved productivity. By 1980 it increased to 11 million units, about half of which were exported, making Japan the biggest producer of compact cars.

● **Shipbuilding Growth**   Since eclipsing England in 1956, Japan has become the world's leading shipbuilder, although tonnage is now showing a decline due to an excess of ships and more market share being taken by such emerging shipbuilding nations as South Korea.

● **Electrical Manufacturing Growth** From the '50s to the '60s, production of TVs, refrigerators, washing machines and other home appliances soared, and TVs were established as a stable export. VCR production since the latter half of the '70s has also accelerated.

● **New Machine Industry Advances** Demand for computers in many fields has increased as society moves into the information age, and output is steadily growing, as is that for NC machines capable of producing highly sophisticated parts. There is also increased demand for and production of industial robots.

■Vehicle Production

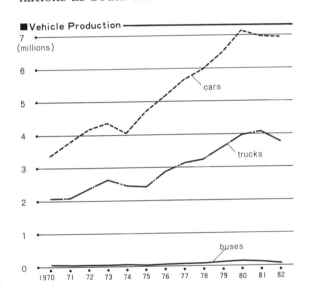

■Steel Ship Construction

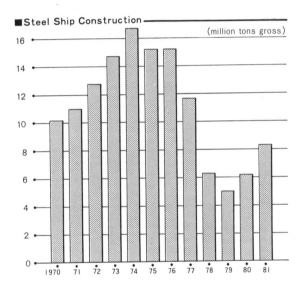

■Electrical Machines Production

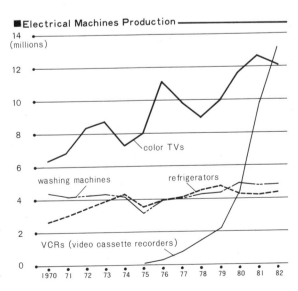

■Computer/Industrial Robot/NC Machine Production

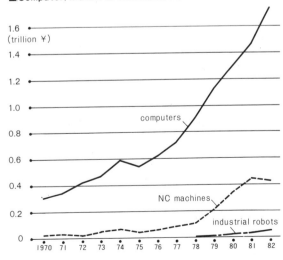

● The Chemical Industry

Ethylene, the first product derived from raw gasoline and itself the base for numerous other products is, in its production, a good index to the condition of the petrochemical industry. The industry made great strides during the nation's years of high economic growth when emphasis was on heavy chemicals, coming to stand second only to America. Lately, however, it is having to cope with a severe depression triggered by price hikes from the two oil crises and competition from the new petrochemical industries of the oil-producing nations.

The medical drugs industry has certain features not found in other chemical industries of the processing type. One is the huge volume of shipments. Another is the advances into the field by such outside interests as the food products industry and foreign enterprises.

Sales of medicines rose as medical costs went up due to a higher incidence of adult diseases, and provided the industry with a long period of prosperity. Now, however, it is facing difficulties due to government steps to lower medical costs and competition from firms that have developed new biotechnological techniques.

■ Ethylene Production

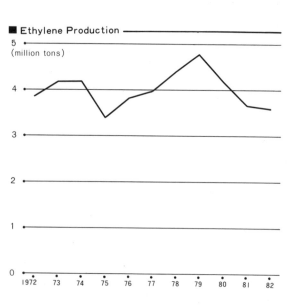

■ Fertilizer Consumption

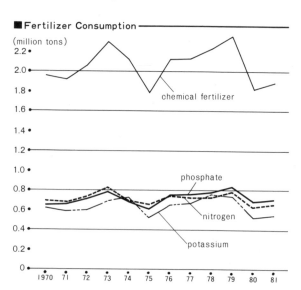

■ Major Cloth Production

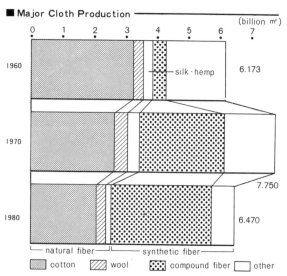

■ Medical Drugs Production

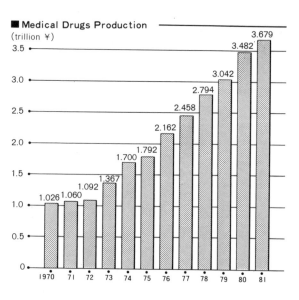

● **Construction Investments** For a number of years now, investments have fallen. Reasons include (1) government cutbacks on money for flood control/aforestation, road construction, sewerage projects and other public works, (2) extreme caution in undertaking large-scale civil engineering or architectural projects due to the slow economic growth induced by the two oil crises, and (3) low housing construction as a result of high land prices and tightened income.

● **Housing Starts and Housing Problems**

In 1972 housing starts topped 1,850,000 but fell to 1,500,000 in 1978, with those for homes going from 750,000 in 1973 to 500,000 in 1983. Figures are also down for government housing and tract developments, while rental homes have increased but, on average, floor-space has decreased 3-4m².

Low housing starts does not mean an end to the housing problem. Homes here compared with those in America and other advanced nations do not measure up in terms of space and other amenities, mainly because of overly high land prices.

■ Workplaces And Employees In The Construction Industry

Field	Workplaces (1980)	Employees (1980)	Field	Workplaces (1980)	Employees (1980)
Construction Industry	550,798	4,969,163	Masonry/Brick/Tile/Blocks	11,419	54,296
All-round Construction	212,580	2,836,762	Plaster	39,558	163,624
Gen. Civil Eng. & Arch.	15,485	564,755	Roofing (excld. metal)	6,439	32,430
Civil Engineering	62,338	1,131,901	Sheetmetal/Hardware	27,577	86,200
Pavement	5,158	121,170	Painting	22,083	140,436
Dredging	479	9,123	Other	21,922	177,699
Architectural Constr.	30,895	431,302	Repair/Installation	105,218	1,032,203
Wooden Architecture	98,225	578,511	Electrical	47,671	396,877
Other (excld. installation)	233,000	1,100,198	Communications/Signals	5,630	106,379
Carpentry	72,666	164,612	Pipes (excld. well-digging)	43,801	395,962
Foundation/Concrete	17,978	158,076	Well-digging	1,787	11,254
Steel Frame/Rods	13,358	122,825	Other	6,329	121,731

■ Number of Newly Built Houses

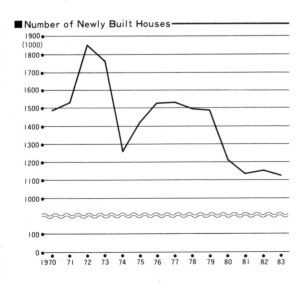

■ Construction Investments

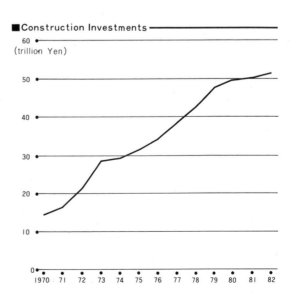

BUSINESS AND SERVICE INDUSTRIES

● **Wholesale and Retail** In terms of stores, the retail-wholesale ratio is higher than in western nations and indicates the need to streamline the distribution system. The sales growth-rate in the wholesale sector fell due to the oil crisis and recession but has recently been climbing and is most apparent in the oil and electronics parts sectors. The retail sales-rate, however, is showing a decline due to no substantial growth in consumer income.

● **Department Stores and Supermarkets** Since the oil crisis of the '70s, department store sales have fallen and were eclipsed by supermarket sales in 1972. Though super-markets have rapidly proliferated, their sales too have been dulled by intensified controls on opening large-scale stores, the lack of consumption and changing consumption patterns.

● **Restaurant Growth** Some 80% of all eating and drinking establishments are small affairs with 1 - 4 employees and are relatively easy to start up. Higher consumer income and lightened household labor have provided more chances to eat out, so that the number of bars and restaurants of all types has increased, especially western-style restaurants.

■ Wholesale And Retail Stores/Employees/Annual Sales

Stores (1000)

0 200 400 600 800 1000 1200 1400 1600

Employees (1000)

0 1000 2000 3000 4000 5000 6000

Sales (trillion Yen)

0 50 100 150 200 250 300 350 400

☐ wholesale ☒ retail

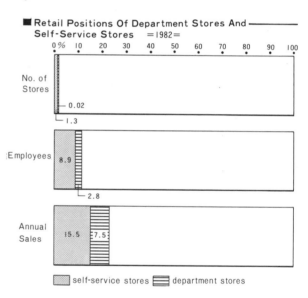

■ Retail Positions Of Department Stores And Self-Service Stores = 1982 =

0% 10 20 30 40 50 60 70 80 90 100

No. of Stores — 0.02 — 1.3

Employees 8.9 — 2.8

Annual Sales 15.5 7.5

☐ self-service stores ▤ department stores

■ Eating Establishments (excluding bars) By Type/Number/Employees/Annual Sales

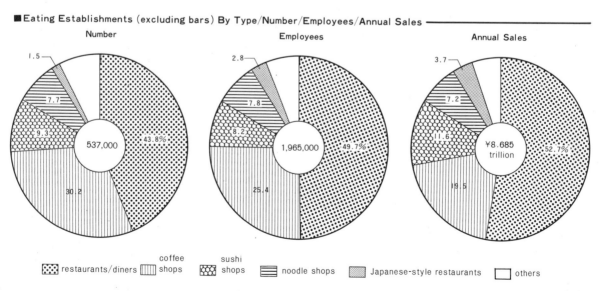

Number — 537,000 — 43.8% — 30.2 — 9.3 — 7.7 — 1.5

Employees — 1,965,000 — 49.7% — 25.4 — 8.2 — 7.8 — 2.8

Annual Sales — ¥8.685 trillion — 52.7% — 19.5 — 11.6 — 7.2 — 3.7

▨ restaurants/diners ▥ coffee shops ▨ sushi shops ▤ noodle shops ▨ Japanese-style restaurants ☐ others

● Service Industry Growth

Higher personal income and more leisure time find more money being spent on travel and eating out, so that the service industry shows a high growth-rate even though some sectors are not doing as well as others. Building and information services are on the increase, while movie theaters and public baths are declining. Information services and business services for industry are expected to gain in importance, and private enterprises will have a bigger hand in the enrichment of education, medical care and welfare.

● Trends in Advertising Outlays

Money spent on advertising is not at the rate it was during the high economic growth period but still accounts for some 1% of the GNP. By industry, the biggest spenders are in the publishing, service and entertainment sectors etc.

By medium, the largest outlays after TV are on newspaper ads. Magazines reached a peak in publications in 1983 and, by their diversity, have become a big advertising medium. Other ad forms include direct mail, billboards and inserts.

■ Newspaper Advertising (1983)

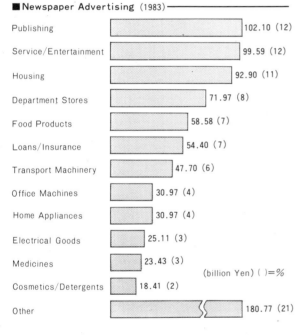

Publishing	102.10 (12)
Service/Entertainment	99.59 (12)
Housing	92.90 (11)
Department Stores	71.97 (8)
Food Products	58.58 (7)
Loans/Insurance	54.40 (7)
Transport Machinery	47.70 (6)
Office Machines	30.97 (4)
Home Appliances	30.97 (4)
Electrical Goods	25.11 (3)
Medicines	23.43 (3)
Cosmetics/Detergents	18.41 (2)
Other	180.77 (21)

(billion Yen) ( )=%

■ Radio Advertising (1983)

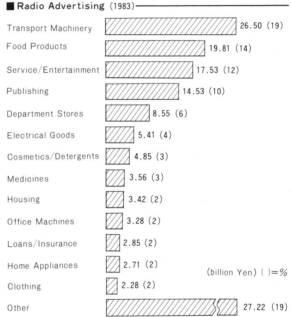

Transport Machinery	26.50 (19)
Food Products	19.81 (14)
Service/Entertainment	17.53 (12)
Publishing	14.53 (10)
Department Stores	8.55 (6)
Electrical Goods	5.41 (4)
Cosmetics/Detergents	4.85 (3)
Medicines	3.56 (3)
Housing	3.42 (2)
Office Machines	3.28 (2)
Loans/Insurance	2.85 (2)
Home Appliances	2.71 (2)
Clothing	2.28 (2)
Other	27.22 (19)

(billion Yen) ( )=%

■ Advertising Money By Medium

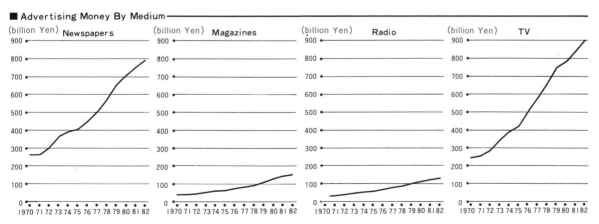

WORLD TRADE

● **Economy and Trade** As a populous island nation endowed with few natural resources, Japan has been able to develop its economy by importing raw materials and exporting finished goods, upping exports to overcome domestic economic slumps.

● **Exports and Trade Friction** "Trade Dependency" as an index to the importance of trade in a nation's economy shows that exports account for 13% of Japan's GNP, almost twice that of resource-rich America, though still lower than the 20% level for Germany, England and Canada. Serious trade friction, however, has arisen from the tendency of exports to be concentrated geographically and, in specific categories (VCRs, semi-conductors, cars, etc.), overwhelmingly, while imports are, to an extreme, materials and fuels, thus creating a trade structure of few imports of machine goods from the advanced nations. Also, despite strong demands from abroad for liberalizing farm products, such steps are precluded by the need to preserve domestic agricultural industries.

To dispel trade friction, the emphasis on finished-goods exports should shift and overseas production be vigorously pursued.

■ **Trade Dependency Of Major Nations**

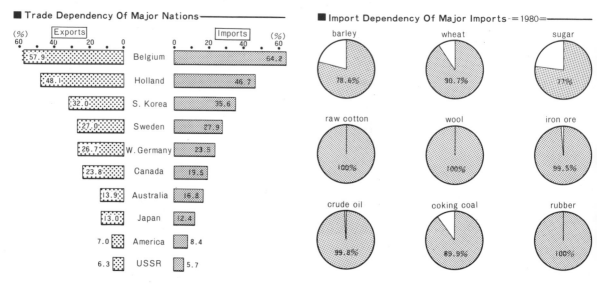

■ **Import Dependency Of Major Imports = 1980 =**

barley 78.6%	wheat 90.7%
sugar 77%	raw cotton 100%
wool 100%	iron ore 99.5%
crude oil 99.8%	coking coal 89.9%
rubber 100%	

■ **Import-Export Structure Of Commodities**

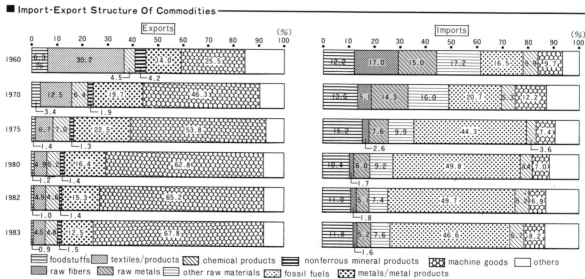

foodstuffs   textiles/products   chemical products   nonferrous mineral products   machine goods   others
raw fibers   raw metals   other raw materials   fossil fuels   metals/metal products

● Geographic Trade Features

Japan's exports go nearly everywhere, but almost 30% to America, with but 5% to the nearest contenders. Over 65% of exports to the U.S. are machine goods, and cars occupy such a big share that voluntary export restraint is observed. Imports are high in meat, soybeans and other food items, while the finished-goods rate has topped 50% due to increased imports of aircraft and semi-conductor parts. Exports to the EC are mainly machine goods, with cars and electrical machines a big share. Imports are chemical products, machine goods and foodstuffs.

Imports from Australia and Canada are coal, mineral ores, other raw materials and foodstuffs, creating an unfavorable trade balance, a phenomenon also happening with oil-rich Saudi Arabia, the U.A.E., Indonesia and Iran. Trade and economic co-operation with S.E. Asia are also up. Chemical products and machine goods for the heavy chemicals industry are exported, and light-industry items and raw materials imported. Yarn and textile imports are so high that quotas may be imposed. Also up are machine goods from S. Korea, Taiwan and Hong Kong. To the USSR, exports are mainly machine goods and steel, with low imports; to China, machine goods for steel plants. Oil is 40% of imports from China.

■ Japan's Import-Export Trade By Nation And Value =1982=

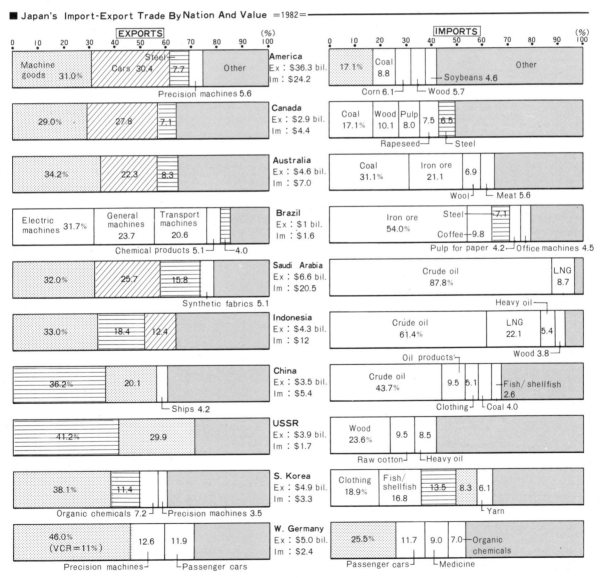

POPULATION

● **Population And Population Structure**

The population is now 120 million, which puts Japan 7th after China, India, the USSR, America, Indonesia and Brazil. A limited land area gives Japan a high density.

The population will continue to grow, reaching about 130 million by 2010, then decreasing so that by 2080 it will settle at about the present level.

The population structure, when viewed by age group, shows that as the birthrate rose, the shape was that of a pyramid; but after 1950 it became more eggshaped as the birthrate fell, so that by 1980 the predomi-

nant segment was those in their 30s-40s.

Youths 15 and under are at present on the decline, and will constitute 17% of the total population. Those 65 and over, however, are increasing and by 2040 will account for 22%. One out of every 4.5 persons will be old.

In general, the population of an advanced nation ages and that of a developing one gets younger. U. N. studies show that as the world population grows, those 65 or over will go from 214 million (8.5% in 1980) to 1.121 billion (13.7% in 2025).

■ Population Growth

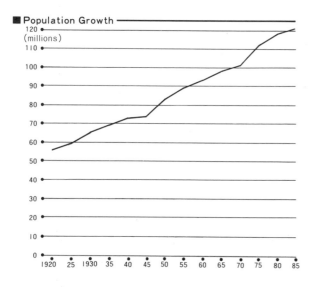

■ Population Structure By Age Group

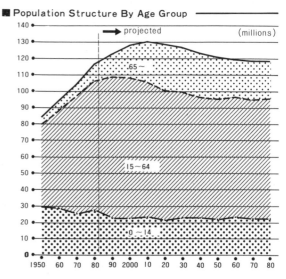

■ Birth/Death/Natural Increase Rates

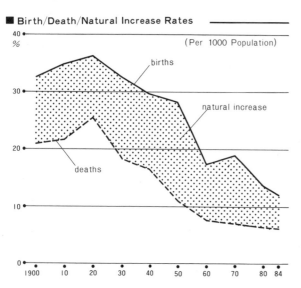

■ Population And Density Of Major Nations

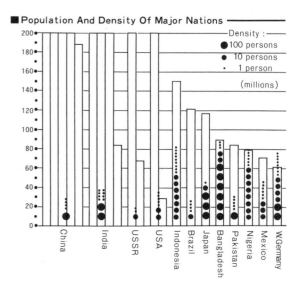

POLLUTION/TRAFFIC ACCIDENTS/FIRES

● **Pollution**   By category, complaints around 1970 were mainly those regarding air and water quality.   More numerous now are complaints about noise. Fewer now cite noise from factory or construction sites, and more complain about such neighborhood disturbances as piano playing, air-conditioners and late-night bars.

● **Traffic Accidents**   After 1970, when dead and injured reached 16,765 and 980,000 respectively, the figures fell. Now they are on the rise again.   Many traffic fatalities occur in the cities and involve pedestrians and cyclists.   Fewer who are 15 and under

and more 60 or over are killed, while people in the 16-29 age group make up one-third of the total, of which over 40% were cyclists.

● **Fires**   The occurrence of fires rose from 17,000 in 1948 to 73,000 in 1973, afterwards declining a bit so that in 1982 the number stood at about 60,000.   Many occur from winter to spring, with the most common hours being between 2:00-3:00 a. m.

In addition, each year many people are injured by such natural phenomena as storms, typhoons and earthquakes.

■ Pollution Complaints

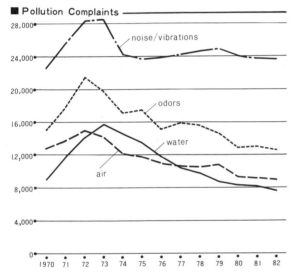

■ Traffic Accidents

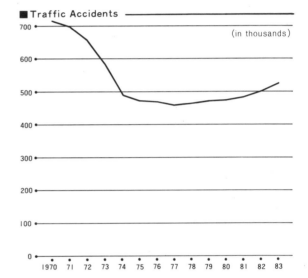

■ Time of Traffic Accidents Resulting in Death/Injury

grade / Time	Preschool Infant	Nursery	Primary 1—3	4—6	Jr. High	Total
0 ～ 2	45	21	1 / 39	1 / 37	6 / 155	8 / 297
2 ～ 4	20	12	24	19	5 / 83	5 / 158
4 ～ 6	36	1 / 21	41	62	2 / 134	3 / 294
6 ～ 8	5 / 206	1 / 319	13 / 1 364	3 / 697	13 / 1 601	35 / 4 187
8 ～ 10	19 / 1 280	20 / 1 737	13 / 1 296	8 / 925	5 / 1 503	65 / 6 741
10 ～ 12	29 / 2 413	17 / 1 579	9 / 1 657	4 / 1 082	3 / 885	62 / 7 616
12 ～ 14	33 / 2 136	20 / 2 129	13 / 2 777	4 / 1 697	9 / 1 638	79 / 10 377
14 ～ 16	40 / 2 964	36 / 3 875	47 / 6 332	15 / 2 813	9 / 1 978	147 / 17 962
16 ～ 18	48 / 3 373	47 / 5 183	40 / 7 809	22 / 4 737	15 / 3 599	172 / 24 701
18 ～ 20	23 / 1 468	20 / 1 709	17 / 2 285	7 / 2 045	23 / 2 429	90 / 9 936
20 ～ 22	11 / 358	4 / 259	8 / 378	10 / 391	11 / 969	44 / 2 355
22 ～ 24	7 / 135	1 / 60	2 / 92	97	5 / 285	15 / 669
Total	215 / 14 434	167 / 16 904	163 / 24 094	74 / 14 602	106 / 15 259	725 / 85 293

(1983)   (upper figures : deaths/lower : injured)

■ Fires and Their Causes

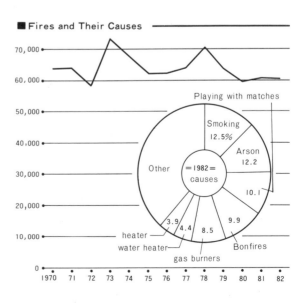

FINANCE

● Deficit Funding／Deficit Bonds

Tax revenues fell due to the recession so that in FY 1975 special government bonds began to be issued in earnest. As revenues went on falling, deficit bonding rose, with the result that national bond dependency went to 39.6% in FY 1979. Although it dropped to 25% in FY 1984, it still compares unfavorably with America's 21.5%, England's 5.2% and West Germany's 13.1%.

● Bond Interest Payments and the Tax Burden
Bond dependency growth has had a serious effect on expenditures. Bond-redemption and interest payments in FY 1984 went to 18%, topping outlays for regional finance and public utilities. As a graphic illustration of the enormity of the interest payments, hourly expenditure is something like one billion yen (FY 1984).

A problem common to the task of financial reconstruction is the tax burden rate. Although on the rise, it is relatively low when compared on an international scale. In FY 1984 it was 24.2%. In FY 1982 it was 27.1% for America, 43.9% for England and 30.9% for West Germany.

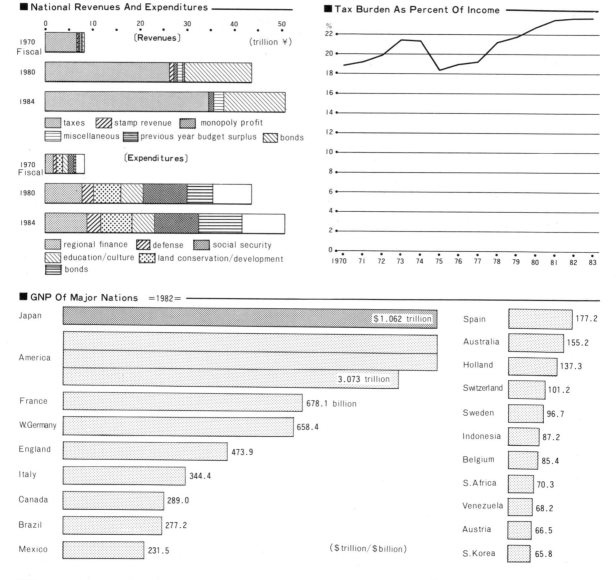

■ National Revenues And Expenditures

(Revenues) (trillion ￥)

1970 Fiscal / 1980 / 1984

☐ taxes ▨ stamp revenue ▦ monopoly profit
▤ miscellaneous ▥ previous year budget surplus ▨ bonds

(Expenditures)

1970 Fiscal / 1980 / 1984

▨ regional finance ▨ defense ▨ social security
▧ education/culture ▨ land conservation/development
▤ bonds

■ Tax Burden As Percent Of Income

■ GNP Of Major Nations ＝1982＝

Japan	$1.062 trillion
America	3.073 trillion
France	678.1 billion
W.Germany	658.4
England	473.9
Italy	344.4
Canada	289.0
Brazil	277.2
Mexico	231.5

Spain	177.2
Australia	155.2
Holland	137.3
Switzerland	101.2
Sweden	96.7
Indonesia	87.2
Belgium	85.4
S.Africa	70.3
Venezuela	68.2
Austria	66.5
S.Korea	65.8

($ trillion/$ billion)

PRICES/HOUSEHOLD FINANCE

● **Price Trends**   The harsh price spiral set off by the 1973 oil crisis has now stabilized due to government measures and the lessons business learned from it. The trend to stabilized prices has been even more evident when compared to other nations.

● **Price Index and Its Nonperception** Despite price stability, strong complaints are often voiced about the difficulty in making ends meet, a complaint traceable to the gap between the consumer price index and its actual perception in daily life.

The index, a set formula drawn up by the government, is but a faint reality for the ordinary worker strapped with a heavy mortgage and feeling taxed to death. A Swiss survey on living expenses in major cities of the world found that after Lagos, Nigeria, Tokyo is the most expensive and difficult city in which to live.

● **Tightened Household Finances** Real income over the past 10 years has averaged a 1.6% annual growth, while taxes, insurance premiums, mortgages and other payments have risen, so that savings are down. Average educational expenses per household are over ¥60,000 monthly, absorbing some 20% of household budgets. Entertainment outlays account for about 10%.

■ Consumer Price Index Of Major Nations

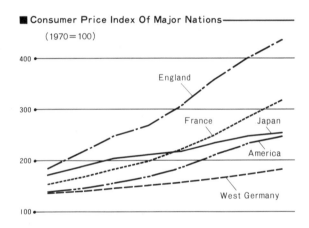

■ Wholesale And Consumer Price Indexes

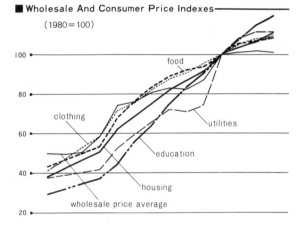

■ Monthly Income/Expenditures Of Workers' Households

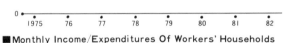

■ Index Of Charges (Tokyo)   1934−36=1

Item Year	Water 15 m²	Postage 1 p.c.	Rail 1 km	News- paper 1 month	Bath 1 adult	Barber adult
1960	156.3	333.3	153.8	398.9	330.0	474.5
1965	187.5	333.3	176.3	495.5	516.7	907.3
1970	187.5	466.7	269.2	775.0	740.0	1 255.1
1975	293.4	666.7	326.9	1 753.2	1 825.3	3 673.4
1980	632.8	1 333.3	715.0	2 439.3	3 783.9	6 088.6
1983	945.3	2 666.7	849.4	2 693.4	4 730.1	7 111.9

SOCIAL SECURITY

● **Social Security Benefits** Medical care and old-age benefits account for over 80% of outlays, with welfare, aid-to-dependent children, unemployment and other programs receiving less than 20% of overall expenditures.

Japan has a rapidly aging population, which means that as the number of old people increases, expenditures for medical care and the aged will also increase.

The imbalance in the distribution of benefits will thus continue for some time.

Catching up with the level of advanced nations was, until now, the aim of the system. The degree to which that has been accomplished is open to debate, but the fact that substantial progress has been made is undeniable.

The system is, by necessity, financed through taxes and insurance premiums, and needs revamping to create a more equitable balance between the burdens and the benefits so that it will be on a more solid foundation as the nation heads into the 21st century and an aging society.

■ Social Security Expenditures

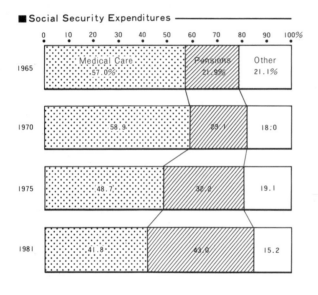

■ Victims Of Major Contagious Diseases

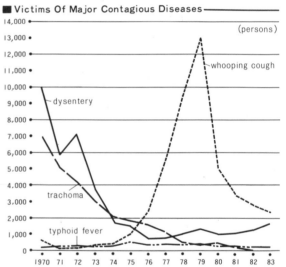

■ Prevalency Rate Of Illness

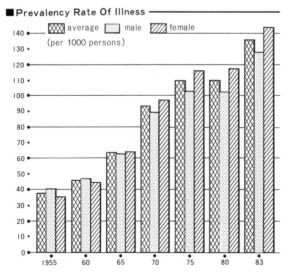

■ Food Poisoning Incidence

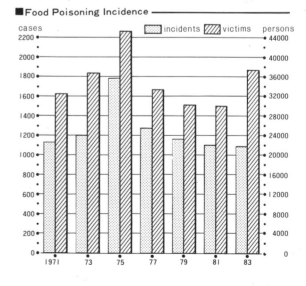

● **Prevalence of Sickness/Death Rate By Cause** The rate of illness is higher now than it was around 1955. This is not due to any general deterioration in health but is simply because medical attention is now more readily available thanks to the medical insurance system. Also, the aged among the population are increasing, and they, more than the young, are apt to suffer injury and illness and require prolonged periods of treatment.

The aging of the population is also clearly shown in mortality tables. Tuberculosis was at one time the nation's biggest killer.

Nowadays, however, few contract it and even fewer die from it.

The top three killers now are malignant tumors (cancer), cerebral-vascular disease (stroke, etc.), and heart disease (myocardial infarction, etc.), which are mainly adult disorders afflicting middle-aged or older persons.

Mortality tables also show a rise in accidental deaths. Excluding accidents that involve chidren in the 1-4 age group, traffic deaths are highest for all age groups, and are followed by drowning among school children aged 5-14.

■Major Causes/Numbers Of Deaths ——————————————————————————— (per 100,000)

YEAR	1st Cause	No.	2nd Cause	No.	3rd Cause	No.	4th Cause	No.	5th Cause	No.
1950	Tuberculosis	146.4	Cerebral-vascular disease	127.1	Pneumonia & Bronchitis	93.2	Gastroenteritis	82.4	Malignant tumor	77.4
1960	Cerebral-vascular disease	160.7	Malignant tumor	100.4	Heart disease	73.2	Old age	58.0	Pneumonia & Bronchitis	49.3
1970	Cerebral-vascular disease	175.8	Malignant tumor	116.3	Heart disease	86.7	Accidents	42.5	Old age	38.1
1980	Cerebral-vascular disease	139.5	Malignant tumor	139.1	Heart disease	106.2	Pneumonia & Bronchitis	33.7	Old age	27.6
1983	Malignant tumor	148.3	Cerebral-vascular disease	122.8	Heart disease	111.3	Pneumonia & Bronchitis	39.3	Accidents	24.8

■Food Intake By Major Food Groups　(per person/day)

	1965	1970	1975	1980	1982
Cereals { rice	349.8g	306.1g	248.3g	225.8g	218.2g
Cereals { wheat	60.4	64.8	90.2	91.8	95.9
Potatoes	41.9	37.8	60.9	63.4	61.0
Oils & Fats	10.2	15.6	15.8	16.9	18.3
Beans	69.6	71.2	70.0	65.4	67.2
Green/Yellow Vegetables	49.0	50.2	48.2	51.0	58.7
Other vegetables	170.4	199.1	198.5	200.4	201.1
Fruits	58.8	81.0	193.5	155.2	159.7
Seaweed	6.1	6.9	4.9	5.1	5.0
Seasonings/beverages	87.8	126.7	119.7	109.4	114.6
Fish/Shellfish	76.3	87.4	94.0	92.5	90.2
Meat	29.5	42.5	64.2	67.9	70.8
Eggs	35.2	41.2	41.5	37.7	40.0
Milk/Dairy products	57.4	78.8	103.6	115.2	124.2

■Nutritional Intake　(per person)——————————————

		1965	1970	1975	1980	1982
Calories	kcal	2184	2210	2226	2119	2136
Protein	g	71.3	77.6	81.0	78.7	79.6
Animal Protein	g	28.5	34.2	38.9	39.2	40.0
Fat	g	36.0	46.5	55.2	55.6	58.0
Animal Fat	g	14.3	20.9	26.2	26.9	28.2
Carbohydrates	g	384	368	335	309	306
Calcium	mg	465	536	552	539	559
Iron	mg	—	—	10.8	10.4	10.8
Vitamin A	IU	1324	1536	1889	1986	2120
Vitamin B_1	mg	0.97	1.13	1.39	1.37	1.38
Vitamin B_2	mg	0.83	1.00	1.23	1.21	1.26
Vitamin C	mg	78	96	138	123	132

EDUCATION

●**The Spread of School Education** School education is so widespread that it ranks among the highest in the world. Enrollment at the primary and secondary levels is nearly 100%, while that for higher education averages 30% (40% for boys, 20% for girls.)

A breakdown by attendance and advancement shows that attendance for compulsory grades (1st-9th) reached 100% early on. For kindergarten it has been at 64% since 1975, and advancement to high school at 92-93% for boys, 94-96% for girls since 1976, while that for universities reached 30% for boys, 43% for girls in 1978. The 94.

3% advancement onto high school in 1982 dropped slightly in '83, suggesting a limit has been reached. A drop in continuation onto university/junior college suggests a rethinking about advanced education.

●**Re-evaluating the Education System** Now that education has spread so widely the time has come to re-examine its content, quality and duration, as well as education in the home and in society at large, taking into consideration the deep concern and diverse opinions of all.

■ Rate Of School Attendance In Major Nations

Name of Country	Year	Primary and Secondary levels	Higher education	Name of Country	Year	Primary and Secondary levels	Higher education
Japan	1980	97	30.2	E. Germany	1981	94	30.4
S. Korea	1981	96	17.5	USSR	//	101	21.2
China	//	83	1.3				
India	1978	51	7.5	Canada	1981	99	37.0
Philippines	1980	92	26.1	America	1980	99	57.1
Egypt	1980	63	14.8	Mexico	1981	89	14.6
				Argentina	//	93	23.6
England	1980	91	20.1	Brazil	//	77	11.5
W. Germany	//	79	27.6				
France	//	96	25.5	Australia	1980	99	25.8
Italy	//	84	27.1				
Sweden	1981	91	36.8				

■ Student Numbers In Japan Enrollment

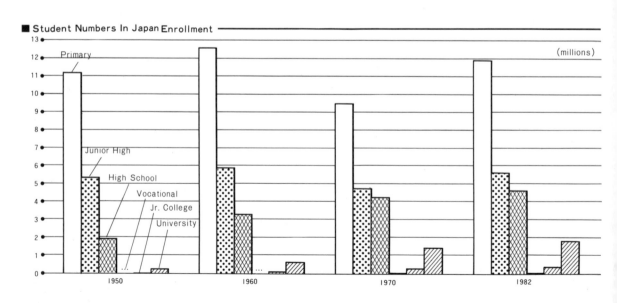